THE
SERPENT
OF
PARADISE

*The Incredible Story of
How Satan's Rebellion
Serves God's Purposes*

ERWIN W. LUTZER

MOODY PRESS
CHICAGO

© 1996 by
ERWIN W. LUTZER

All Scripture quotations, unless indicated, are taken from the *New American Standard Bible*, © 1960, 1962, 1963, 1968, 1971, 1972, 1973, 1975, 1977, and 1994 by The Lockman Foundation and are used by permission.

Scripture quotations marked KJV are taken from the King James Version.

Parts of chapter 4 were adapted from Erwin W. Lutzer and John F. DeVries, *Satan's Evangelistic Strategy for This New Age*. Published by Victor Books, 1989. Used by permission.

ISBN: 0-8024-2720-2

1 3 5 7 9 10 8 6 4 2

Printed in the United States of America

*In honor of our Lord and Savior Jesus Christ,
who "disarmed the rulers and authorities
[and] made a public display of them,
having triumphed over them through Him"
(Colossians 2:15).*

CONTENTS

FOREWORD

I t was the fall of 1964. I was sitting in a classroom of the Free
University of Amsterdam listening to a lecture by my profes-
sor, G.C. Berkouwer. It was an unusually hot day in Holland,
and the room had no air-conditioning. I found myself allowing
my mind to wander as I gazed out the window, staring at the
ducks paddling on a canal next to the street. My reverie was suddenly interrupted and my mind snapped to attention when Pro-
fessor Berkouwer uttered a simple, terse sentence.

I don't know how many words I've heard spoken in lectures
and sermons in my life, but I am sure the number is in the millions. I am likewise sure that I have forgotten the vast majority of
those words. But I still remember the words Dr. Berkouwer
spoke in this single, terse statement: "There can be no sound theology without a sound demonology." What Dr. Berkouwer was
getting at is that if biblical revelation is taken seriously we must
take seriously what Scripture teaches concerning the satanic
realm.

In America we've all heard the expression "Buddy, do you
have a match?" In Dutch the expression is "Mijnheer, heeft u en
lucifer?" ("Mr., do you have a match?"). The Dutch word for
"match" is "lucifer," the very word used in Scripture for Satan. I
do not know how the Dutch word for a match came from such an
etymological derivation, only that it does. Surely, however, there
is a lexicographical link to the New Testament assertion that
Satan masquerades as an "angel of light." Satan does not appear

to us as the grotesque and hideous figure he is, or as he is depicted in folklore, or as caricatured by Halloween costumes. Rather, Satan is metamorphic. He likes to appear *sub species bonum*, "under the auspices of the good." He is, as he is introduced in Genesis, the most crafty and subtle of creatures. He is the quintessential con artist working his scams via camouflage.

Satan's two most effective ploys are (1) to get people to underestimate him à la Lt. Columbo, so that he can lure us into a hidden snare, or (2) to overestimate him that we may be so intimidated by him that we are paralyzed by his threatening power. He loves it if we deny his existence and thereby ignore him or if we elevate him to the level of God and become preoccupied with him. We may not be able to be possessed *by* him but we surely can become obsessed *with* him.

When Erwin Lutzer asked me to write this foreword he was most gracious. He knew that I do not share his views on certain matters of eschatology that are treated in this book and that I would disagree with him on a few details. But if I had to agree with another author on every detail of his book before I endorsed it I would probably not be able to endorse any book save the Bible. Likewise, no one would ever be able to endorse any of my books.

There are three chief reasons I am pleased to endorse this book. (1) What unites Erwin Lutzer and R.C. Sproul in theology is far greater than what divides us. (2) I have found a profound appreciation for Erwin Lutzer as a man, a Christian, and a defender of the faith. We all know people with whom, as soon as we see them, without a word being uttered, we feel an instant rapport. When I see Erwin my spirit is buoyed. (3) Perhaps most important is that I found this book a veritable treasury of biblical insight. One of the banes of being a theologian is that most Christian books I read contain little information that I haven't read many times before. Yet I learn from repetition, as I guess I am a slow learner. This book, however, is filled with lucid insights I have never considered. It was a sheer delight to learn so much at one sitting.

When I am at home in Orlando it is my custom to arise each morning at 4:00. My body clock has its own alarm system. This morning I opened my eyes at exactly 3:58. By 4:15 I was reading this manuscript. I was facing the task of giving four lectures scheduled to begin at 9:00 A.M. I usually spend the early hours preparing my lectures. Today I had to forego that luxury, as I became so absorbed by this book. In my judgement it is positively brilliant. It is the best treatment of the person and work of the enemy I have ever read. It is not simply an exercise in abstract theology: it is a feast of spiritual insight that I personally need to digest. I can hardly wait to read it again. It not only stimulates the mind but is poignantly edifying to the soul.

R. C. Sproul
Orlando, 1996

1

PUTTING THE
DEVIL IN HIS PLACE

This book is a modest attempt to put the devil in his place. When Lucifer (whose name means "light bearer") rolled the dice, gambling that he could do better by being God's enemy rather than God's friend, he set in motion a moral catastrophe that would reverberate throughout the universe. You and I have been deeply affected by his decision made in the ages long ago.

What may not be widely known is that Lucifer was already defeated the moment he sinned. He was defeated *strategically*, since as one of God's creatures he would be forced to depend upon God for his continued existence. Any power he would exercise would always be subject to God's will and decree. Thus moment by moment he would suffer the humiliation of knowing that he could never be the ultimate cause of his existence and power.

To clarify, I don't mean to simply say that for every move he would make, God would make a counter-move. That was true of course; but the situation for Satan would be more ominous. As will be shown in the chapters of this book, he cannot even now make his own first move without God's express will and consent!

Let us boldly affirm that whatever mischief Satan is allowed to do, it is always appointed by God for the ultimate service of and benefit to the saints. William Gurnall, after encouraging believers to hold fast to the assurance that God is watching Satan's every move and will not let him have the final victory, writes, "When God says 'Stay!' [Satan] must stand like a dog by the table while the saints feast on God's comfort. He does not dare to snatch even a tidbit, for the Master's eye is always upon him."[1] And so it is; our Master's eye is ever upon him. After his first act of disobedience, his failure and doom were sealed.

Though he could never have predicted it, at the Cross Lucifer would be defeated *spiritually*, for there Christ was guaranteeing that at least a part of fallen humanity would be purchased out from the kingdom of darkness to share in the kingdom of light. The fact that creatures who had fallen into Satan's trap would eventually be exalted above the angelic realm he once led was more than he could bear. But bear it he must.

Finally, when he is thrown into the lake of fire, he will be defeated *eternally* in that he will be forever cast away from the divine presence. There in shameful agony he will unendingly contemplate his foolishness in standing against God. His humiliation will be public, painful, and endless. Even as you read these words, he is a hapless player in the drama that he himself set in motion. And there is nothing he can do to change the outcome.

In medieval times, the devil was often pictured as a long-tailed, cloven-hoofed jester with two horns and a red suit. He looked the part of a clown; he often was pictured as a loser in the conflicts of the ages. Cartoons depicted him as a buffoon whose very presence was an affront to humanity.

Let us not think that the people of the Middle Ages actually believed that the devil looked idiotic. They knew, even as we do, that he was actually an evil spirit who was both powerful and fearsome. The purpose of the caricatures was to strike at his most vulnerable point, namely his pride.

They wanted to convey that the devil was a fool to mount opposition to God. Though he is a being of immense intelligence, he was decidedly unwise to rebel against his Creator. The medievals made him out to look stupid because, despite his power and staggering knowledge, he was stupid indeed. They knew that the devil was both real and powerful; they also knew that he was misguided and defeated. Thus Luther insisted that when the devil persists we should jeer and flout him, "for he cannot bear scorn."

The medievals might be faulted for paying too much attention to the devil and often mixing biblical truth with legends and superstitions. But we must commend them for their vigorous belief in the existence of the Prince of Darkness. Our age, in contrast, must be faulted for giving him only scant recognition, or even worse, for giving him the kind of recognition he craves.

When the devil persists we should jeer and flout him.

We can be thankful for a recent article in *Newsweek* that observed that those who are "born again" take the devil seriously.[2] We who believe in the trustworthiness of the Bible are not guilty of disbelieving in his objective existence. We, above all, should take the devil seriously. Very seriously.

But our sincerity does not guarantee that our conception of the devil is accurate. I believe that the renewed emphasis on the work of Satan by evangelicals, in, say, the last twenty years, has been, for the most part, helpful. Surely we are much better equipped to stand against our enemy because of the writings of those who have warned us of his schemes and reminded us of our resources to fight against him. As a young pastor, I was introduced to spiritual warfare by those who knew more about our enemy than I.

However, along with much helpful advice, some distortions have crept into our thinking that could play into the devil's hands. Though they do not expressly state it, some writers imply that Satan can act independently of God; they speak as if God becomes involved in what the devil does only when we ask Him to. Because Satan is the "god of this world," they think this means that he can be free to make his own decisions, inflicting havoc wherever and whenever he wishes.

I respectfully disagree.

Of course, all evangelicals concur that the devil will eventually be defeated; but for now, some teach he is free to do pretty much whatever he pleases in the world. The Satan of many of the so-called deliverance ministries is one who calls his own shots and wields his power, limited only by the broad parameters God has laid out for him. Satan, according to this theology, sets his own agenda and is free to harass us without much interference from the Almighty.

We need to be reminded of Luther's words that even "the devil is God's devil." We have forgotten that only when we know who God is can we know who the devil is. Blessed are those who are convinced that the prince of this world has become the slave of the Prince of Peace.

History has examples of those who wrote about the devil without a careful study of the Scriptures. These writers have, for good or for ill, shaped much of our thinking about Satan. Let us remind ourselves of a few who were most influential.

WHICH DEVIL?

Dante

Dante (1265–1321), who takes a tour of the lower regions in his classical masterpiece *The Inferno,* has the horrific experience of seeing demons torment the pitiful occupants of hell. These demons patrol a river of boiling pitch, giving sinners the exact punishment they deserve. With hooks and sharp claws, the demons attack any sinner who tries to escape or flout their authority. The punishment of these people is meted out with unerring accuracy: Each of the nine regions is designated for a particular sin, and each person receives retribution according to what he or she has done, with the hypocrites in the lowest circle. The demons delight in tormenting those who have committed the most hideous offenses.

This portrait of Satan, which dominated much of medieval thinking, was not based on the Bible but popular folklore. Although it engendered a lively belief in the existence of Satan and his demons, it misread the devil's role in the world. The myth that the devil is the tormentor in hell is just one more way of giving the Evil One the kind of recognition he craves. Worse still, Dante neglected the New Testament doctrine of salvation and substituted a salvation of works. Though Dante is rightly considered one of the greatest writers of all time, we could wish that he had either studied the Bible more thoroughly or had written about matters other than theology.

Milton

Milton (1608–1674), in his epic poems *Paradise Lost* and *Paradise Regained,* recovered a biblical portrait of Satan. Belief in the devil had begun to wane in worldly Shakespearean England, and he must be credited with reviving a biblical belief in Satan's existence. Though his theology also was at times deficient and his imagination became the basis for much of what he wrote, these poems cover the whole gamut of salvation history. Milton argues that the angels had free will, and thus evil became a possibility. In fact, he would say that moral goodness is impossible without free will; God, however, turns the evil to good by teaching us wisdom and faith through our trials and suffering.

Milton made Lucifer both alluring and repulsive; both a hero and a villain. Satan is depicted as powerfully attractive; Milton intended the reader to be caught up in admiration, to feel the tug of temptation toward this terrible, self-indulgent Prince of Darkness. Gradually, however, the true nature of Lucifer is revealed and the seductive power of evil becomes clear.

Yet Milton retained some of Dante's folklore. Satan rebelled, says Milton, because he would "rather reign in Hell than serve in heaven." When he returns to hell from the Garden of Eden, having succeeded in corrupting man, he is greeted with a chorus of hisses. Though he claims to have shaken the throne of God, that claim turns out to be a lie. Although the other fallen angels are "groveling and prostrate" on the lake of fire, Satan calls them to arms, addressing them by their angelic titles.

Milton combined the theology of the Bible with Christian tradition and a lively imagination. We might not agree that free will alone can account for Satan's fall; and we most assuredly should not agree that the devil is already in hell, or that he shall ever be a king there. But Milton has given us a compelling account of the struggle between good and evil, the struggle between Satan, Adam, and Christ. His vivid descriptions became the stuff of artists, novelists, and preachers.

Belief in the devil was making a comeback.

Then came the Enlightenment.

Goethe

The demise of the devil in Western thought can be traced to that era where belief in the supernatural world began to retreat in the face of humanistic learning and scientific discoveries. Soon the devil became a figment of an older superstitious era. Since the God of Luther and Calvin was replaced by a sunnier, more tolerant God, it was generally believed that His universe could have no place for an independent evil being.

If you think that Faust made a pact with the devil and then discovered to his horror that he had been tricked into losing his soul, you are correct, but only if you are thinking of the medieval versions of the story. Though Faust apparently was an actual historical figure with magical powers, the legends that grew up around him gave rise to many fanciful stories about his stunts, trickery, and, of course, pacts with the devil. One version has him dying during a mysterious demonstration of flying in 1525. Folklore, which was often widely believed, said that he was carried off by the devil.

But there is another *Faust*, a more popular version written by the German Enlightenment scholar, Goethe (1749–1832). Here, more than one hundred years after Milton, Faust encounters a different devil, a being who has some elements of the Christian view but no longer a creature to be feared. In fact, according to Goethe's play, it is Faust who outwitted the devil!

Goethe's Mephistopheles (the devil) is a very complex figure, even the creator of the angels. And though he appears in opposition to God, he is a serious distortion of the Christian devil: He is portrayed as a being who invites the reader to face the multiplicity of reality. He certainly is not to be feared.

When Faust makes a pact with Mephistopheles, the devil promises that he will be Faust's servant in this world if Faust will be his servant in the world to come. Mephistopheles lures Faust into sensuality by playing upon his lust for a young woman, Gretchen, who falls in love with him. Confused and demoralized, Faust eventually follows the path of least resistance and fulfills his fantasies by going to Gretchen's bed.

But—and this is important—Faust's lust eventually is transformed into real love. Thus Mephistopheles has not destroyed Faust but has actually done the good that he despises. As the play ends, there is a struggle for Faust's soul. But Faust outwitted Mephistopheles because he had learned to love.

Faust, therefore, was saved—not from sin, but from sensuality and dry intellectualism. And he was saved, not by Christ, but by his own efforts at striving. Faust discovered that serving Mephistopheles had both liabilities and rewards. Making a pact with him need not have serious consequences.

Goethe's Mephistopheles fits well within the framework of contemporary America. The devil turns out to be primarily whatever we want him to be. We can be in league with him without fearing that we shall actually lose our souls. This is a symbolic devil of a weaker, comic sort.

Our age believes in a tame devil. He is eager to serve our need to explain the existence of evil and willing to be a symbolic description of the horrors we struggle to understand. He is a devil who is best for us; a devil who is our servant; a devil who shares his power, predicts our future, and helps us develop our potential. He is a devil of horoscopes, Ouija boards, and Dungeons and Dragons; a devil of the New Age Movement, who helps us get in touch with "masters of wisdom" and affirms our own enlightened humanity.

According to a *Newsweek* poll, at least 25 percent of Americans believe that the devil is really only a symbol of man's inhumanity to man. Of those who say they believe in the devil, only a small percentage believe they have ever been tempted by him. "Among Christians," says *Newsweek*, "only the born-again reveal a robust sense of the devil's presence."[3]

Such views are compatible with those mainline Protestants and Catholics who have, in the words of Kenneth Woodward, "exorcised the Devil from their working vocabulary."[4] We can talk of the devil just as long as he is not thought of as an independent, evil personality. His value is symbolic, descriptive, and speculative.

Sociologist Robert Muthnow suggests that whether or not you believe that the devil has objective existence often depends upon your social class. "Look at the parking lot outside any church," he says. "If you see Lexuses and Cadillacs, you won't hear Satan preached inside. If you see a lot of pickup trucks, you will."[5]

Why This Book?

This book attempts to give an overview of the career of Satan and his interaction with the Almighty. It traces his fall from an exalted position to his defeat by Christ and to his demise in everlasting shame and contempt. It attempts to prove that Satan always loses, even when he "wins." Best of all, it shows that we who have been translated from the kingdom of darkness into the kingdom of light are able to stand against him.

My first premise is that *God has absolute sovereignty in His universe.* That means that even evil is a part of the larger plan of God. Of course, I do not mean to imply that God either does evil or approves of it. However, I do mean that by virtue of His role as creator and sustainer of the universe, God is the ultimate (though not the immediate) cause of all that comes to pass.

I am convinced that unless we grasp how the devil fits into God's scheme of things, we will find it more difficult to stand against his conspiracy against us personally and his influence within our culture. How we perceive our enemy will largely determine how we fight against him.

We can have a proper theology of the devil only if we have a proper theology of God. Only when we stand in awe of God will we find it unnecessary to be in awe of Satan. Therefore, this is a book about Satan, but it is also a book about God's power, God's program, and God's purposes in the world. The greater our God, the smaller our devil.

Satan ... was defeated the moment he chose to sin.

We must live with the unshakable confidence not only that God will win in the end, but that He is actually winning even now, day by day. We do not have to wait until Satan is cast into the lake of fire before we can rejoice that our enemy is crushed. I shall take pains to show that he was defeated the moment he chose to sin against the Almighty. My central affirmation is that *although Lucifer rebelled that he might no longer be God's servant, he still is!*

Many years ago the title of a popular book by J. B. Phillips reminded us that *Your God Is Too Small*. Perhaps in our time, another book should be written titled *Your Devil Is Too Big*. Our devil is too big if we are fascinated with him; our devil is too big if we think we have to fulfill a vow to him; our devil is too big if we are victims of a curse that has been put upon us. Our devil is too big if we live in fear that our future is in his hands.

One writer offered this helpful illustration: A single quarter lifted to the eye can obscure the blazing light of the sun, a star whose diameter is 865,000 miles. Just so, Satan, if we let him, can cause us to block out our vision of God. He can give us the terrifying optical illusion that, at least in this life, he is just about as big as God.[6] Remember, Satan gets more power as we give it to him!

Satan is just as strong as we believe him to be. Because the Israelites believed the city of Jericho to be unconquerable, *it was*. The citizens of Jericho saw it quite differently: they were terrified of the Israelites and were puzzled as to why they did not come and claim their inheritance forty years earlier. Indeed, Joshua and Caleb knew that God had "removed the protection of the city" (Numbers 14:9). It was not the strength of the city but the unbelief of the Israelites that postponed the victory. By ascribing to the city more might than it had, the Israelites conferred upon it the right to rule. Just so, if we believe Satan is invincible, he will conform to our expectations. That is why we must never see Satan without seeing God.

My second premise is that *God uses our conflict with Satan to develop character.* These struggles give us the opportunity of having our faith tested. Our spiritual war is a classroom where we can learn about the deceitfulness of sin and the chastisement of God—along with His grace and power. God could have banished Satan to another planet or cast him immediately into the lake of fire. But He chose to use the devil, to give him a role to play in the divine drama. God knows that we must fight before we can celebrate. We must learn before we are approved. God permits Satan's temporary reign, the Puritans used to say, "to increase the saints' eternal joy."

God would not throw us into the conflict if He did not also

give us the resources needed to stand against the enemy. That is not to say that we always avail ourselves of the assets that are ours as Christians. I have known my share of failure in battling the Prince of Darkness. But I interpret these failures as my responsibility—a responsibility I share with other believers who are a part of the same body of Christ.

Several chapters in this book are devoted to what we have come to call "spiritual warfare." I attempt to show how we can recognize the most common of Satan's wiles against us. Best of all, we must affirm with confidence that we are in a winnable war. We are up against a being who has all the limitations of a creature.

Only the Bible can help us evaluate the conceptions of Satan popularized by Dante, Milton, and Goethe. In the Scriptures, we are confronted by an enemy of God who must nevertheless do God's bidding. We are exposed to a being who will never reign or torment people in hell; nor is he a devil who is the figment of our imagination, a being whom we can outwit if we are clever enough.

The biblical portrait of Satan is that he does indeed have great power, but that it is always limited by the purposes and plans of God. It is a picture of a proud being who has already been humbled. It is the picture of a being whose greatest asset in his war with us is our own ignorance.

I shall have failed you, the reader, if you do not have greater faith in God's victory after reading this book. I pray I shall be given the wisdom to remind us that Satan is great to us, but not great to God. We must stand in awe of a God who can use a rebel to glorify His name.

We must never see Satan without seeing God.

2

THE STAR THAT
BIT THE DUST

Y ou were in Eden, the garden of God."
With this single statement, we enter into a world that lies
just beyond our imagination. It is a world of beauty, peace,
and unity. It is a world so unlike what we've experienced that it
strains the limits of our fancy. To see the gardens in the Schon-
brunn palace of Vienna is wonder enough; just imagine the "garden of God"!

Yet here in a realm beyond our grasp, a glorious creature
chose to take a cosmic gamble that would backfire. He tripped a
series of dominoes whose interrelationships were unknown to
him. His act, once accomplished, would reverberate for all of
eternity; the entire universe would shudder, reeling from the
shock. Even now, you and I feel the painful effects.

This was the father of all gambles; it was the opening gambit
of a drama—not a comedy to be sure, but a tragedy of megapro-
portions. God would use it for His glory, of course; indeed, there
is evidence that this was part of a larger plan. But that does not
lessen the brutal impact of that fateful day when one of God's
creatures embarked on a path whose trajectory would carry him
ever further from his privileged position of influence and fulfillment.

To uncover the details we turn to the Bible, the book that tells us of events in the invisible realm that we could never discover on our own. The curtain is pulled back, and we are introduced to the characters of the drama. As we look more carefully, we realize that we too are on stage, participating in the conflict of the ages.

The Creature He Was

Who was this creature who exchanged peace for war? Who was this misguided one who thought he was trading servanthood for kingship? His name was Lucifer, or "shining one." He was the "light bearer." He had no natural light of his own but was expected to reflect the light and glory of God.

God would never create a being who was as great and beautiful as He Himself is. Any created creature would of necessity fall short of the limitless perfections of the Almighty. Lucifer was therefore much less than God, but evidently he was the "best" the Almighty could do.

The Bible invites us to part the curtain, to glimpse the whys and wherefores of Lucifer's rebellion. Two prophets of the Old Testament tell the story of a being who is more than simply a human king; they introduce us to that world where the grand, cosmic gamble was made.

Both Isaiah and Ezekiel tell the same story, but from slightly different points of view. Both prophets pronounce woes on the proud kings of their day. Both remind the monarchs that God will not let them get by with their arrogance and rebellion. He will bring them down from their lofty perch of cynical elitism.

But then the prophets launch into descriptions that could not apply to any human being; they describe a more powerful being who stands behind the kings of this world. They tell us of a creature who once possessed awesome beauty, but now has become thoroughly evil. It is as if they are looking back through the corridor of time and seeing cosmic history. We are introduced to a creature who lived in the garden of God but ended in the abyss of contempt and humiliation.

Let us let Ezekiel speak for himself:

Again the word of the Lord came to me saying, "Son of man, take up a lamentation over the king of Tyre, and say to him, 'Thus says the Lord

God, "You had the seal of perfection, full of wisdom and perfect in beauty. You were in Eden, the garden of God; every precious stone was your covering: the ruby, the topaz, and the diamond; the beryl, the onyx, and the jasper; the lapis lazuli, the turquoise, and the emerald; and the gold, the workmanship of your settings and sockets, was in you. On the day that you were created they were prepared. You were the anointed cherub who covers, and I placed you there. You were on the holy mountain of God; you walked in the midst of the stones of fire. You were blameless in your ways from the day you were created, until unrighteousness was found in you. By the abundance of your trade you were internally filled with violence, and you sinned; therefore I have cast you as profane from the mountain of God. And I have destroyed you, O covering cherub, from the midst of the stones of fire. Your heart was lifted up because of your beauty; you corrupted your wisdom by reason of your splendor. I cast you to the ground; I put you before kings, that they may see you. By the multitude of your iniquities, in the unrighteousness of your trade, you profaned your sanctuaries. Therefore I have brought fire from the midst of you; it has consumed you, and I have turned you to ashes on the earth in the eyes of all who see you. All who know you among the peoples are appalled at you; you have become terrified, and you will be no more."'"
(Ezekiel 28:11–19)

If you ask why Bible scholars have for centuries believed that Ezekiel begins by discussing the king of Tyre but ends with a report about Lucifer, you would find that it is because this description cannot refer to any human being. The king of Tyre never was "full of wisdom and perfect in beauty," nor was he ever "the anointed cherub who covers," much less "blameless in all [his] ways."

The King of Tyre [was never] "the anointed cherub who covers."

Therefore, to make sense of the passage, we must either spiritualize it or assume that Ezekiel was speaking of a being who stands behind the king of Tyre. Since the Scriptures teach that Satan rules the nations, it is reasonable to assume that Ezekiel is speaking about that angelic creature who once deserved the descriptions given in this passage but then arrogantly fell into rebellion. He who was the apex of creation would eventually live in eternal shame and contempt.

Let us consider this description more carefully. "You were in Eden, the garden of God; every precious stone was your covering: the ruby, the topaz, and the diamond" (v. 13). This Eden was not the garden of Eden, for this is a description of mineral beauty, not vegetation. It is a garden bedecked with jewels and every form of extravagance, a paradise that is a suitable home for one who possessed creaturely perfections. Lucifer was God's masterpiece, a showpiece whose presence brought glory to his creator. This was God at His best.

The Duties He Performed

What did Lucifer do in those glorious days when the universe enjoyed the tranquillity of perfection? We read, "You were the anointed cherub who covers, and I placed you there. You were on the holy mountain of God; you walked in the midst of the stones of fire" (v. 14).

What did Ezekiel mean by the phrase "the anointed cherub"? Perhaps it is a general reference to service in the kingdom of God. Barnhouse, in *The Invisible War*, suggests that the phrase refers to a priestly function associated with the cherubim, who even now lead the worship of heaven. The wings of a cherub, you might recall, were outstretched on the top of the ark of the covenant. Confirming this interpretation is the expression "his sanctuaries," apparently a reference to worship (v. 18).

If this interpretation is correct, it means that Lucifer evidently directed and orchestrated the worship of other angels. He received the worship of the angels beneath him and passed it on to God above him. None of the adoration was to be diverted along the way. God alone deserved all that was accorded Him.

We cannot be certain where Lucifer had his abode. Barnhouse believes that his sphere was this earth. After all, one of Lucifer's desires was to "ascend into heaven." Though he had access to the throne of God, earth was his habitat. That was where he was assigned to carry out his priestly duties.

Most other scholars believe that Lucifer's primary residence was near the throne of God in heaven. Ezekiel says he was "cast . . . to the ground" (v. 17), perhaps intending us to understand that he was cast on to the earth after he sinned. Whether on earth or in heaven, it seems clear that Lucifer was a cheerleader for the Almighty.

How long did he enjoy this privilege? We don't know, but it might have been for millions of years, or perhaps for only a short time. Milton suggests that it was the creation of Adam and Eve that caused Lucifer to be overcome with jealousy, and that he sinned shortly after their creation. Whatever, until he sinned, he existed to serve God, without weariness, struggle, or competition. He was God's worship leader, the director of choirs and coordinator of praise.

If only he had known how fortunate he was!

The Gamble He Took

We are shocked and perplexed by this simple statement, "You were blameless in your ways from the day you were created, until unrighteousness was found in you" (v. 15).

Unrighteousness was found in you!

With that breathtaking comment we have a description of how sin entered the universe. This is an inspired commentary on the origin of evil—unrighteousness was found in a being that moments before had been perfect!

What was this sin, this unrighteousness? In a word, it was arrogance. "By the abundance of your trade you were internally filled with violence, and you sinned. . . . Your heart was lifted up because of your beauty" (vv. 16–17). His beauty and position led to hardened pride. In the New Testament, Paul wrote that a novice should not be ordained to ministry so that he will not "become conceited and fall into the condemnation incurred by the devil" (1 Timothy 3:6).

The city of Tyre boasted of its trade; just so, Lucifer took pride in his duties as a manager of God's affairs. Specifically, instead of passing all of the praise to God, he began to keep some of it for himself. Like a trader who keeps a bit of the profits that cross his desk, so Lucifer would hold back some of the worship, enjoying what he thought was his share. Perhaps he believed it was only proper that God receive most of the worship and praise, but not all of it. Why should the Almighty not share that glory with His creatures, particularly that one who was His brightest and best?

Here we encounter a theological puzzle that has taxed the best minds for centuries: How can an unrighteous choice arise out of the heart of a righteous being? Even more to the point: Why would a perfect creature become dissatisfied in a perfect world? This was a being who evidently was fulfilled in serving God; if he was satisfied, why rebel?

Most theologians attribute his decision to free will. They say that he had an option before him, and as a free creature (even a perfect one), he always had the potential of going astray. Perhaps that is part of the story, and we must agree that Lucifer was not coerced by God or other angels to do what he did. But we are still left with a puzzle. Why would such a creature *want* to defy God? Even if he had free will, we cannot understand why he would exercise his option.

Perhaps the best answer is that there is no answer. Or, to put it more accurately, there is no answer that we as humans can discern. God has an answer—and perhaps someday He will give us the missing piece of the puzzle. Until then, we just don't know why Lucifer suddenly allowed unrighteousness to erupt in his heart.

What we do know is that Lucifer was self-deceived, thinking that rebellion was necessary if he were to put his own interests first. He failed to grasp that even if he were motivated by self-interest, obedience to God would still be best. To put it differently, God's best for him and his best for himself were actually one and the same.

Lucifer's bad judgment is a warning to us. We must never think that our obedience is best for God, but not best for us. When God commands us to obey Him, He not only has His best interests in mind but ours too. That is why we are never wiser than when we choose to follow God's will, whatever the cost.

Against all rational probability, Lucifer pitted his will against that of God. Consumed with jealousy and burning with a desire for recognition, he set out to do what he wanted to do rather than what God wanted him to do. Whatever momentary satisfaction he gained from his decision, it would be outweighed by the everlasting contempt that he would have to endure. But he wasn't thinking that far ahead.

The moment he rolled the dice he was doomed to disappointment. His future was gambled in a slot machine that paid no dividends. He had miscalculated the power and intention of God.

The Motivation He Had

We have already learned that Lucifer chose his own way because of a thirst for recognition. Even today as I write these words, he still thirsts for what he now knows he can never have. Like the proverbial sailor who drinks salt water and then discovers to his horror that he has only increased his burning desires, so Satan drinks only to increase his frustration and hasten his doom.

Isaiah tells a similar story. He begins by giving a warning to the king of Babylon; then, like Ezekiel, he describes the being who stands behind the king. He gives five goals that Lucifer staked out for himself. If it is true, as the New Agers teach, that whatever the mind can believe the mind can achieve, Lucifer is to be commended for his ambitions. Each statement begins with the lofty phrase "I will."

> *I will ascend to heaven; I will raise my throne above the stars of God, and I will sit on the mount of the assembly in the recesses of the north. I will ascend above the heights of the clouds; I will make myself like the Most High.* (Isaiah 14:13–14)

No small aspirations here. These cries of progressive desire are the yearnings of cynical arrogance.

"I will ascend to heaven." Sometimes we say that the birds fly "in the heavens." But beyond the atmosphere, we have the stellar heavens, where countless stars make their rounds, and there is also a third heaven, which is the very dwelling place of God.

Lucifer had already had the privilege of visiting the courts of the highest heaven to offer praise to God. Now when he says he wants to "ascend to heaven," he means that he would like to take God's place. He wants to sit on God's throne, if he could. Not satisfied with earth, he longs for a permanent place in heaven.

He wants to ascend, not to serve but to rule. He does not

want to worship, but to confront; he does not want to obey, but to rebel. Little does he realize that this desire for the highest of all ascents will eventually lead to the lowest of all descents. He who had enjoyed the glories of heaven will descend into the very horrors of hell.

"I will raise my throne above the stars." Elsewhere we learn that the stars are often symbolic of angels (Job 38:7). Lucifer already had authority over them, but it was a delegated authority. He longed for independent power. He wanted to be worshiped and feared. Weary of taking orders, he now wanted to give them according to his whim rather than God's plan.

"I will sit on the mount of the assembly in the recesses of the north." A mountain frequently is symbolic of a kingdom or nation (Isaiah 2:2). Lucifer longed for God's authority to rule over a kingdom. He was obsessed with having a dominion of his own. More accurately, he wanted to steal territory that belonged only to God.

"I will ascend above the heights of the clouds." God's glory is manifest in a cloud (Exodus 16:10). This Shekinah glory represented the very essence of God's presence. Lucifer wants to be above the clouds, even above the glory of God, if he could.

"I will make myself like the Most High." Finally his heart is revealed. He would be like God. He saw the glory and honor that God received, and now he wants it all for himself. To be worshiped will be his consuming passion. Please note that his desire was to be *like* God, not to be unlike Him. Ironically, this arrogant desire would make him as much *unlike* God as it is possible to be!

Until Lucifer's blunder, there was harmony in the universe. Every will created by God was obedient to the Divine will. God was the ruler, and His creation responded to the divine initiative. But from now on, there would be opposition to God's instructions. Lucifer would recruit other angels in his assault on God. Then the human race would join those angelic hosts in rebellion. Rather than one unified plan in the universe, there would now be millions of plans, each of them driven by personal ambition. The rule of God would be opposed at every quarter.

What a colossal error in judgment Lucifer made! He rolled the cosmic dice, not realizing that the word *success* had never been written on them. The moment the idea of opposing God entered his mind, he was doomed to fail.

Here was a being who knew God and yet did not believe that God's ways were best. Here was one who was not content with serving, but rather wanted to be served. But alas, he still serves!

WHY THE GAMBLE FAILED

Lucifer, I believe, sincerely miscalculated both the consequence of his decision and God's reaction to it. He suddenly found himself in a predicament that he could not have foreseen. He thought he was in control of his own future, but it soon became clear that his tomorrows would be determined by the very One whom he had so arrogantly spurned. His supposed lurch into freedom was a plunge into bondage.

Lucifer would now learn what all creatures must: We might be able to control our decisions, but we cannot control the results. *Sin triggers the law of unintended consequences.*

Why was he cursed to fail?

He Was Limited in What He Could Achieve

What could Lucifer have hoped to attain when he rebelled against God? He wanted to be like the Most High, but was this even remotely possible?

When theologians describe God, they use three words that begin with the prefix "omni," which simply means "all." For God to be *omni*present means He is everywhere present; to be *omni*potent is to be all-powerful; to be *omni*scient is to have all knowledge. These attributes are the very essence of who God is.

How many of these attributes could Lucifer hope to achieve in desiring to be "like God"? The answer, of course, is none.

He could never be omniscient; that is to say, he would never know everything. He knows that a man is planning to assassinate the president of the United States when he comes to Dallas, Texas, on November 22, 1963. But he does not know whether it will actually happen. The man might change his mind, the gun might jam, or perhaps the motorcade will take a different route at the last moment. God knows exactly what will happen, but Satan will be able to give only an informed guess. Though he knows plans, he does not know the end results. He can influence human decisions, but he can never direct them. His fondest dreams are ever in jeopardy.

That explains why in the Old Testament the mark of a false prophet was that he would sometimes be wrong in his predictions. Often right, but sometimes wrong. Only God can know the future infallibly. Therefore, a true prophet of God would be accurate 100 percent of the time.

And what about omnipresence? Will Lucifer ever be able to fill the whole universe with his presence? Will he be everywhere simultaneously? No, he cannot be. He can travel quickly, but when he is in India, he cannot be in Washington. When he is fighting a battle in Chicago, he cannot be at a prayer meeting in Korea. He will never be omnipresent. True, multitudes of demons are scattered throughout the world doing the devil's work, but all of these fallen angels also can only be in one place at a given time.

What about omnipotence? Lucifer will never be all-powerful. He probably does not even have the power to create a single molecule, much less have the power to create stars, the sun, and the moon. Nor can he hold the universe together by the "word of his power." When he seeks to mimic God's ability to create, he must resort to fakery. No, he will never be omnipotent.

In what sense then can he be "like the Most High"? Only in this: He thought he would be independent. He knew that his accomplishments would always be but a shadow of what God can do. But the joy of knowing that he was now acting without God's approval was worth the risk. He now would only give orders and supposedly not receive them. At least that was the plan.

The irony is that Satan's flaunted independence would in reality turn out to be another form of dependence on the will and purposes of God. True, he wouldn't depend on God for guidance in the decisions he made, but every one of his rebellious acts would be under God's careful direction and control. He could defy God, to be sure, but his activities would always be limited to what God allowed. His independence was hardly worthy of the word. As mentioned in the previous chapter, he rebelled so that he would not have to be God's servant, and yet today he still is!

Later in this book, we will discuss Satan's limitations in more detail. Here, it is sufficient to point out that he cannot afflict Job without divine approval. He cannot harass Saul, except that he is sent to Saul by God. And he cannot give the apostle Paul a "thorn in the flesh" without God determining both its time limitations and severity. This does not sound like independence! In fact, as we shall see later, it is slavery.

If Milton was right in saying that Lucifer preferred to be a king in hell than a servant in heaven, he (Lucifer) was sadly mistaken. Lucifer discovered to his chagrin that in the end he would continue to be God's servant. And, as we shall see, there are no kings in hell!

He who hated servanthood would now become a servant of another sort. Rather than voluntary servanthood, his would be a reluctant servanthood, service with a different motive and toward a different end, but service nonetheless. In the end, he would still exist for God's glory just as much as he did when he and God were in harmony.

Satan was now condemned to a ceaseless existence of misery and restless emptiness. He would ever be driven to despise God and attempt to work against Him. Yet, in the end, he would always be compelled to promote God's purposes. Rather than joy in the presence of God, there would now be eternal humiliation; in the place of the love of God, there would now be God's hatred and condemnation.

Pride caused Lucifer to gamble his privileges away. He took the big risk, thinking that if he could not dethrone God, at least he could set up his own throne somewhere in the universe.

He had underestimated God and overestimated himself.

He Was Limited in What He Could Foresee

Lucifer knew that there would be some consequences to his anarchy, but he had no idea what those would be. Remember, until that point there had been no example of rebellion in the universe. He could not learn from the mistakes of others; and once he had crossed the line, it was too late to retreat from his blunder. More important, he could not foresee the coming of Christ to redeem man, nor could he predict his own demise in the eternal lake of fire.

He didn't know that only one-third of the angels would

choose to join his rebel cause (Revelation 12:4 says that the dragon's tail "swept away a third of the stars of heaven"). If he assumed that all those who were under his authority would side with him in his bid for independence, he had to live with his disappointment.

Think of it. For every angelic being that honored him, two kept giving honor to God! Perhaps Satan was surprised at how well heaven functioned without his supervision and authority. No matter how confidently he exercised his newfound power, he was only partially successful.

For a time, he could only brood about his mistake. All he could do was to wait for God to take the next step.

He Was Limited in Damage Control

Though we are not explicitly told, there is little doubt in my mind that Lucifer greatly regretted his decision the moment it was made. He had stepped through an unknown doorway in the hope that it would open to a bright new future, not knowing there was a chasm on the other side. Now having experienced sin firsthand, he knew that he had just picked the short straw in the greatest gamble of his career. He had spun the wheel, not realizing that God controlled its every rotation. No matter where it landed, he would always have to be the loser—a loser for all of eternity.

He quickly learned that it is not gratifying to set up a rival kingdom only to discover that it must of necessity fail. However pleasant independence might be, it does not help much when you are independently *defeated*, independently *tormented*, independently brought to *shame*.

If only he had known! He had boarded the wrong train; but now that he was defiled, he had to take it all the way to the station. Repentance was impossible—for several reasons.

First, Satan was and is incapable of repentance, since repentance is a gift of God given to humans in whose hearts God is already at work. For Satan to repent would mean there would be something good in him, but no such virtue can be found. He was now thoroughly evil, irredeemably wicked. And God has chosen to abandon him to his well-deserved fate.

As we have learned, a perfect Lucifer found evil within himself; but now that the corruption was complete, good would never again rise within him. When he had creaturely perfections, he was capable of evil; but once he was contaminated, he would never again be capable of good. The corruption would be complete, irreversible, and total. Sinning would now become a moral necessity.

Second, and most important, even if Lucifer did repent, he could not be redeemed, for no sacrifice was made for his sins. Christ bore only the sin of human beings, not angelic beings. "For assuredly He does not give help to angels, but He gives help to the descendant of Abraham. Therefore, He had to be made like His brethren in all things, that He might become a merciful and faithful high priest in things pertaining to God, to make propitiation for the sins of the people" (Hebrews 2:16–17).

With no atonement available, Lucifer's adversarial behavior was now irrevocable, permanent, and incapable of being rescinded. From now on, his sojourn in the universe would be in a straight line all the way into an eternity of shame and humiliation. For him, there was no second chance.

Lucifer learned an important lesson: A creature can make a mess, but he cannot straighten it out! The law of unintended consequences would have to play itself out throughout all of eternity. Only God can, if He wishes, contain or reverse the aftermath of disobedience.

He Was Limited in Understanding God

God's primary attribute is His holiness. Lucifer, who professed to want to be like God, would actually be as far from this God-likeness as it is possible to be.

We don't know how much God revealed to angelic creatures, but Lucifer, I think, should have known God well enough to realize that He will not share His glory with another. The higher Lucifer aspired to ascend, the further he would of necessity fall.

Did he misjudge God, thinking that His love would eclipse any possibility of stern judgment? We do not know, of course, but keep in mind that Lucifer had only seen God's perfect love. The concept of justice simply did not exist. As long as there was no disobedience in the universe, there was no need for the demonstration of God's anger. Lucifer did not foresee the lengths to which God is willing to go to preserve His honor.

Lucifer thought he knew God, but there was much more that he had to learn. If he had simply trusted what he could not understand and believed what he could not come to know on his own, the future might have been different.

Now that he knew more about God, it was too late.

He Was Limited in Understanding the Difference Between Time and Eternity

Lucifer should have known that no brief exaltation can ever make up for an eternity of humiliation, no moment of worship can ever make up for eternal contempt, no thrill in time can ever make up for the torment of eternity. One hour in hell will make the thrill of opposing God fade into eternal oblivion.

Here is a lesson for us. No decision can be considered good if eternity proves it to be bad. To put it another way, no decision in this life can ever be good unless it is good for eternity. Only a being who knows the future and the past can prescribe what is best for us. We make judgments in time; only God can reveal the judgments of eternity.

From now on Lucifer would win small battles but be forced to lose the war. If only he had taken God more seriously, he would not have underestimated the Almighty's capacity for unerring punishment. If the greatness of the sin is determined by the greatness of the being against whom it is committed, Lucifer had made a colossal mistake.

GOD'S RESPONSE

Where was God in all of this? As always, He was working "all things after the counsel of His will" (Ephesians 1:11). The fall was no surprise to Him. Indeed, the Almighty had created Lucifer with the full knowledge that he would rebel; thus Lucifer's fall was a part of a grand plan.

If we ask why some of the angels sided with Lucifer and others maintained their relationship with God, we find the answer in the mystery of God's eternal purposes. In the New Testament, the angels who didn't fall are called the "elect angels" (1 Timothy 5:21 KJV). They evidently were preserved from sinning by God's decree. The other angels fell voluntarily, no doubt, but nevertheless were also fulfilling a divine plan. The fall was but the first of many scenes in an extended drama.

God had anticipated this in the ages of eternity past. Long before He chose to create so much as a single angel, Lucifer and his future doom was already foreknown and, we might say, ordained. God never learns anything new. He does not have to wait for an event to happen to know its details. He knows all things accurately in advance.

God now had several options.

He could have exterminated Lucifer, crushing him with raw power. Or He could have banished him to another planet. There in a concentration camp in a dark corner of a far-off galaxy, Satan and his demons could have brooded over the foolishness of their decision. Then again, God could have thrown him into the lake of fire immediately. That too would have been fair and just.

But God decided to use Lucifer (whom we shall now call Satan) to demonstrate truths that would have been permanently hidden if evil had not entered the universe. The curtain would rise on a drama acted out on earth in which Lucifer and God, justice and good and evil, would be in conflict.

Here are the rules:

1. *Satan would be given the rulership of the world; he would be allowed to spread his lies.* No doubt he continued to possess the striking characteristics of power and knowledge he had before the Fall, except that now they were perverted. Centuries later Christ would refer to him as "the ruler of this world" (John 12:31; see also 14:30; 16:11). And when Satan offers Christ the kingdoms of this world, Christ does not contradict him!

Satan will never sing again but only howl.

2. *God would give Satan time to see if he could rule his own kingdom successfully.* Could he bring order out of the chaos which he created? Could he actually rule the world if it were given to him?

3. *God would not compromise his own holiness and justice, but would meet Satan on a level playing field, winning a moral and spiritual victory over His adversary.* The Almighty would not just win by power, but by righteousness. The battle would be not only to determine who was the strongest, but who was right and just. Both sides would recruit others to stand with them in the conflict.

He who wished to have his own kingdom will be forced to prove that he can only divide, not unite; he cannot build, but only destroy. He can shout "Let there be light," but he remains shrouded in darkness and hears only the empty echo of his own voice. He cannot endure the truth, but must embrace lies. From now on, says Francis Thompson, Satan will never sing again but only howl.

Though Lucifer is intelligent, he is not wise. And we are born with a drop of his rebellion in our hearts. We stand, as it were, between him and God, caught in the cross fire. Whether we choose the winner or the loser will determine our destiny. For we will get to spend eternity with the God we love and serve. The drama has only begun.

3

THERE IS A SERPENT
IN OUR GARDEN

hanging direction is never easy.

Back in 1995, many investors lost money in an investment organization called New Era. Clients lent the organization money and received a high rate of return—double their money in some instances. Supposedly, hidden donors were matching those funds out of sheer philanthropy. Behind the scenes, however, the generous returns were actually being funded by the acquisition of new investors. The man responsible for the scheme claims that he began with a good motive, but his strategy just "got away from him." For at least a few years, no one suspected trouble because there was enough new money to make payments and keep the operation afloat.

Early on, the founder and director of New Era faced a decision. Should he just admit bankruptcy and face the painful consequences? Or should he continue to plunge ahead, staying afloat by soliciting new money and postponing judgment day? Unfortunately, he chose the second route. When the whistle was finally blown, his creditors were in the hundreds, rather than dozens, and the total loss was in the millions, not the thousands. The longer he prolonged the scheme, the more money was lost and the more people were hurt.

Just so, Satan ignored all the warning bells. Even after his fall, clear thinking should have assured him that greater disobedience would only result in greater torment. Though his doom in hell was sealed from the moment he sinned, if he were to withdraw from the battle, his torments would have been more tolerable. But in his foolishness, the thrill of winning a battle today only postponed a greater pain in the lake of fire tomorrow. And thus we have evil exposed for what it is: The desire to oppose God even with the full knowledge that in the end the Almighty will triumph.

Far from withdrawing, Satan chose to escalate the conflict. Admitting defeat was too humbling; better to forge ahead with sustained rebellion than withdraw from the fray and accept his punishment. He would pretend that illusion is reality; he would call his defeats triumphs. And he would store up more retribution by expanding his rebellious rule.

Other angelic beings were recruited. The idea of creating a rival kingdom, patterned after the angelic realm in which he had served, was a tempting prospect. His hidden desire, of course, was to continue his control of those who were beneath him in the heavenly realms. He who thought obedience to God was slavery now seeks to make others slaves to himself.

As we have learned, other angels followed him. They had been under his authority before he fell, so they chose to follow his lead and join in the growing rebellion. Whether motivated by loyalty or by a craving for their own power and independence, some chose to participate in the great gamble. In return for their rebellion, they thought they would achieve the personal satisfaction of choosing their own path and becoming a part of their own kingdom.

How many angels followed Satan? If it was a third of the angelic realm, the number of rebels might have been in the hundreds of millions. We don't know how many angels were created, but we do know that there are "myriads of myriads, and thousands of thousands" (Revelation 5:11). Whatever the number who sided with Lucifer, and whether they realized it or not, the moment they sinned they became participants in a forced march to destruction.

Satan's next target was human beings. When he watched Adam and Eve being created, he most assuredly thought that they were the strangest creatures he had ever seen. They were made in God's image and had a capacity for fellowship with God that not even the angels possessed. Right from the beginning, Satan knew he would do everything possible to get them to side with him in his attack on God.

Adam and Eve differed from the angels in another way. They could reproduce through procreation. They could multiply by sexual union rather than being individually created. Their offspring would be bound together through blood and have mothers, fathers, brothers, sisters, and cousins.

This solidarity had far-reaching implications for Satan and his minions. When the angels sinned, they did so individually. The decision of one angel did not directly affect the decision of another. Thus, one-third of the angelic host could side with Lucifer and two-thirds retain their loving relationship with God.

Not so among humans. If Adam and Eve were to sin, they would not only contaminate themselves but their offspring. Standing at the head of the race, these would-be parents had the awesome responsibility of making a decision that, for good or for ill, would affect the whole course of human history. Little wonder Satan took a special interest in these strange creatures!

Satan was on hand to hear the instructions God gave to Adam and Eve. He was surprised at the generosity of God. "From any tree of the garden you may eat freely; but from the tree of the knowledge of good and evil you shall not eat, for in the day that you eat from it you shall surely die" (Genesis 2:16–17). They could eat of every tree of the garden except one. Just one no amid a thousand yeses!

Satan waited for the right moment to make his move. He considered his options. The time of the temptation and the means he would use were all-important. This was one opportunity he would not miss!

THE STRATEGY OF LIES

Here we have our first glimpse into the satanic mind and begin to see how this fallen angel operates. As Christ taught, he is "a liar, and the father of lies" (John 8:44). Only in deceit is he consistent. If we would see his signature, we should look for tricky deceptions.

He Lies About Who He Is

He does not come as the devil, the adversary of God. He could have come to Adam and Eve revealing his terrifying fury and evil intentions. But he has no regard for truth in advertising. He comes under a disguise and without revealing who he really is. He changes himself into something he is not to deceive others. He does not come to frighten, but to soothe, to encourage, to instruct.

Though Satan can actualize himself into some kind of a physical body, he cannot create matter ex nihilo, that is, out of nothing. So in this instance he used the body of a beast God had created. He chose a serpent to be the vehicle he would use to tempt our first parents and bring them under his control and authority.

Humans can form sentences, conveying conceptual ideas and speaking of abstract ideas, such as God. In contrast, animals can communicate only with perception, the use of signals designed to beget certain responses. We don't know how Satan communicated with the serpent, but we can imagine that the Evil One told this beast that only he (Satan) had the ability to make the serpent have the same gift of speech as man. Only Satan could make the snake talk.

They eventually get what he wants them to have.

This serpent was likely a beautiful creature, not the detestable beast that slithers on the ground. Far from being afraid of this creature, Eve found herself attracted to it. She thought, of course, that she was simply fascinated by an animal and did not know that she was being captivated by an invisible being who sought her destruction.

Satan has continued to use the same strategy throughout history. He did not come to King David and say, "David, I hate you and have a nasty plan for your life. . . . I want to destroy you, your family, and your kingdom. You have to cooperate and commit adultery with Bathsheba as the first step in the series of dominoes."

Satan never shows us the consequences of psychedelic drugs or alcohol. He skillfully hides the results of pornography, immorality, and dishonesty. Nor does he show us the final state of those who hold to wrong beliefs about the Bible, Christ, and salvation. *His strategy is to give people what they want but to make sure they eventually get what he wants them to have.*

You usually don't try to catch a mouse without a trap. A mousetrap is important because you can use it in your stead to catch your victim while you remain out of view. A trap can hold out the promise of food and fulfillment while keeping the consequences concealed. The mice see only the cheese and do not understand the wire and the powerful spring. Likewise, Satan wants to keep us ignorant of the intriguing dynamics taking place in the spirit world. He wants our circumstances to appear ordinary and his traps unsuspicious. Yet behind the trap is the trapper, and behind the lie is the liar. Paul warned:

> But I am afraid, that, as the serpent deceived Eve by his craftiness, your minds will be led astray from the simplicity and purity of devotion to Christ. For if one comes and preaches another Jesus whom we have not preached, or you receive a different spirit which you have not received, or a different gospel which you have not accepted, you bear this beautifully. (2 Corinthians 11:3–4)

Satan is especially interested in selling another gospel with a sweeter message and a bogus guarantee.

Sometimes Satan uses blatant lies; at other times he mixes truth and error. If we are blind to a part of the truth, we are open to deception. And no one is as blind as the person who has been deceived into believing that he now sees!

He Lies About Who God Is

The first time Satan opens his mouth is to put a question where God had put a period. His first desire is to pervert Adam and Eve's opinion of God. He paints God as mean, uncaring, and threatened by the possibilities latent in the nature of mankind. And so Satan asks this question: "Indeed, has God said, 'You shall not eat from any tree of the garden'?" (Genesis 3:1). And when Eve replies that there is only one tree from which they are forbidden to eat, and that if they should disobey, they will die, the serpent replies, "You surely shall not die! For God knows that in the day you eat from it your eyes will be opened, and you will be like God, knowing good and evil" (vv. 4–5).

God is deceiving you! He is hiding the real reason He does not want you to eat of the so-called forbidden tree; if you do eat, you will be like the Almighty Himself! He wants the glory, not because it is rightfully His, but because He does not want what is best for humanity! God is both a killjoy and a liar.

Don't miss this: Satan got Adam and Eve to concentrate on the one prohibition, the one tree they were not to eat from. He made them blind to the hundreds of exotic trees that lined the walkways of the luxuriant garden. The one negative was used to discredit the countless positives. Satan knew that if he could get Eve to focus on the one thing she did not have, it would rob her of the joy she should derive from all the things she did have.

The one who comes to deceive charges God with deception. The one who cannot speak truth charges God with untruthfulness. Satan lies about himself, making himself to appear harmless. Then he lies about God, making God appear harmful.

And so it is. Even today as believers, we are tempted to look at the world and believe that we have been shortchanged. It is not just teenagers who often think to themselves, "If only I weren't a Christian, think of all the fun things I could do!" Thus, while others enjoy the pleasures of sin, we, poor creatures that we are, must stay at home and be content with the limitless wonders of God's matchless grace. Thus the sons of the King of kings feel sorry for themselves!

Why are we so often lured by temptation? Because we have been conned by the idea that God's way for us is not best. We believe that our obedience might be best for Him, but not for us. But Luther was right when he said that "all sin is contempt of God." His point is that no one deliberately sins but that he thinks wrongly about God. If we really knew God, we would always choose righteousness. Satan's opening gambit is always intended to cause us to think wrongly about the Almighty.

Upon reflection, we know that God was, in fact, displaying His goodness by putting a fence around the tree and saying, "Do not eat!" This was mercy and grace and proof that God cared about Adam and Eve and their future. Whatever restrictions God gives us are for our good and not our detriment.

He Lies About the Benefits of Rebellion

Contradicting God, the serpent says to Eve, "You surely shall not die! For God knows that in the day you eat from it your eyes will be opened and you will be like God, knowing good and evil" (vv. 4–5). God says, "You surely *will* die"; Satan says, "You surely *won't* die."

Notice the conflicting views of God presented to Adam and Eve. On the one hand, God was too good to cause them to die. On the other hand He was too evil to let them achieve their potential. And so it is that the serpent substitutes confusion for understanding.

"You will be like God, knowing good and evil!" That, you recall, is exactly Satan's own dream! He wanted to be like God; he longed to unseat the Almighty and put his throne in the heavens. And now he tells Adam and Eve that if they will but obey him, they will share in his own fantasy.

Surely the Serpent already knew that he would fail in his bid to be like the Most High. His transformation into an evil being gave him self-awareness; most probably it made him painfully alert to his error and the impossibility of winning against God. His own hopes had been shattered, and now he was recruiting Adam and Eve to share in his great eternal failure. He had gambled and lost; now he wanted them to roll the same dice, knowing that they would come up with the same terrifying number.

So they ate, and Satan was proved to be wrong. They did die on the day they ate. Their bodies began to die *physically;* their deterioration would be slow but inevitable. They died *spiritually,* in that they were separated from God. They would also die *eternally* unless God were to intervene.

Satan was right in this respect: Adam and Eve would now have experimental knowledge of evil. They did indeed know "good and evil" for what it was. Their consciences were polluted, and they felt keenly their alienation from God. Corruption had found its way into their souls.

Are the New Agers right in saying that man actually gained through the fall? Was this indeed a fall *upward?* New Agers teach that the serpent and the woman are the redeemers because their act brought about man's enlightenment. It was, after all, the fruit of the tree that gave them this special knowledge which had been hidden from them.

But we don't become like God by having an experiential knowledge of evil. The knowledge that Adam and Eve gained was terrible knowledge. Francis Schaeffer says it is like the knowledge of a child whose mother says, "Don't go near the fire," but the child disobeys, falls into the fire, and spends the next three days dying in agony. The child has learned something—but what knowledge![1]

Every time we sin, we affirm the original lie of Eden.

Adam and Eve were to have knowledge of God and creation. They were given (or could learn) all that was needed to govern the world. It was not evil to seek knowledge, but it was evil to seek this particular kind of knowledge.

THE DECEPTION THAT WORKED

Adam and Eve had the privilege of walking with God in the cool of the garden. There were many trees from which they could eat. If they had had any unmet needs, they could have mentioned those to the Almighty, and He most likely would have given them the desires of their hearts. This was the Paradise of God.

And yet we read: "When the woman saw that the tree was good for food, and that it was a delight to the eyes, and that the tree was desirable to make one wise, she took from its fruit and ate; and she gave also to her husband with her, and he ate" (v. 6). Surrounded by a perfect environment, Adam and Eve sinned.

In a message given at Moody Church, Warren Wiersbe commented on the progression in Eve's decision to believe the serpent.

She *saw* and became *curious.*
She *took* and became a *thief.*
She *ate* and became a *rebel.*
She *gave* and became a *temptress.*

Adam, who was standing with his wife, did not object to her gently plucking the fruit from the tree. And when she had eaten, she shared it with him and he ate with her. They had been introduced to the lie that would now rule the world: *The lie that the creature can be like the Creator.* All other lies are but an extension of this one. Every time we sin, we affirm the original lie of Eden.

The New Testament says Eve was deceived, but Adam was not (1 Timothy 2:13–14). She was deceived because she accepted the serpent as a messenger of God. She thought that the serpent was sent by God to clarify the original revelation. She was willing to accept this "further revelation" even though it conflicted with the earlier revelation—or at least she thought that this latest revelation superseded the former.

How could she have known that this serpent was not speaking for God? Not by asking herself how she felt about it; not by analyzing the luscious fruit to see if it really did look evil, for in point of fact it looked very good. Nor should she have evaluated the vocal inflections of the serpent to see if he was sincere.

Many a person has been deceived because of such subjective feelings about the source of the revelation. False prophets and Satan himself can speak with soothing tones of reassurance and hope. The only sensible recourse for Eve would have been to compare the words of God with the words of the serpent.

Left to our own reasoning, it would make sense to think that since God created the fruit and it looked good, it must be good to eat. Human reasoning is limited and cannot see the big picture; things just might not be what they appear to be.

The tree was not a bad tree, nor did it bear bad fruit. All that God made was good. There was nothing intrinsic about this tree that made it different from other trees. God could have just as easily said, "Don't cross this stream," or "Don't climb this mountain." The tree was simply a test to see if man would obey the voice of God or the voice of the serpent who claimed to speak for God.

If Eve was to be preserved from error, she should have told

the serpent that he was speaking lies. Her responsibility was not to look *within* herself, trying to figure out which way was best, but to look *outside* of herself to an objective revelation.

Today evangelicals still debate whether the Bible alone is sufficient for guidance or whether we need additional revelations and clarifications. Some insist that we should believe visions, prophecies, and dreams if they are not expressly contrary to what the Bible teaches. Others say that such subjective revelations, even if they should be in harmony with the Bible, are a fertile ground for deception.

One evangelical pastor, whose wife left him, returned to the church a few months later with a new and younger bride. Though many in the congregation believed that his divorce and remarriage had disqualified him from ministry, the pastor recounted how he had fasted and prayed in his days of distress and the Lord "told" him that he was to return to lead the same church. Evidently, his board felt that if they removed him from leadership, they would be disobeying what God had revealed. Rather than judge the man on scriptural qualifications, they took for granted the subjective experience of the preacher, who began his explanation with the words, "I sought the Lord and He *told me.*"

Visions of saints, Mary, and of dead relatives might not appear to be blatantly in conflict with the Word of God, but those who accept these as revelations from God deny that the Bible alone is sufficient for a rule of faith and practice. These revelations are said to be needed to give guidance or to stimulate faith. But as history has repeatedly proven, they are often trappings that pervert the gospel and mislead many. Confusing the voice of God with the voice of the devil is not difficult. All that we need to do is give lip service to the finality of the Bible while seeking some additional subjective revelation.

Let us never forget that the very first appearance of Satan on planet earth was one in which he communicated a "revelation" that supposedly was equal to or even superior to the revelation of God. Satan loves to talk. He loves to pretend that he has an inside track on God and that all we need to do is to listen to him and we will have our questions answered.

Though Eve was deceived, Adam ate knowingly. He knew this message was not from God, but he decided to join his wife in the adventure of eating the tasty fruit. Is it not true that forbidden waters are sweeter? Does not independence ignite an excitement that obedience does not?

Like Lucifer before them, Adam and Eve now discovered that nothing would ever be the same again. As for Adam, the ground would be cursed, and he would earn his bread by the "sweat of your face" (Genesis 3:19). Eve was told, "I will greatly multiply your pain in childbirth, in pain you shall bring forth children; yet your desire shall be for your husband, and he shall rule over you" (v. 16).

Adam and Eve now discovered what the devil already knew: The consequences of disobedience are haphazard, unpredictable, and wholly out of our hands. The shame that engulfed them was but the beginning of a life of heartache for them and all of their descendants. Of course, they could not foresee the treachery, violence, and cruelty that would eventually come to planet Earth. They had pulled a stone from a mountain and were horrified to discover that they had begun an avalanche.

THE SCEPTER WAS DROPPED

Adam and Eve deceived by an *animal!*

They had the authority to expel this creature from the garden; they could have banished him from the face of the earth. They could have taken their God-given dominion seriously and said no to the creature's whims. All that, yet they foolishly acted on his suggestions!

Hear it from God Himself: "Let Us make man in Our image, according to Our likeness; and let them rule over the fish of the sea and over the birds of the sky and over the cattle and over all the earth, and over every creeping thing that creeps on the earth" (Genesis 1:26). Man, created in the image of God, had dominion over the world around him. Man was to stand between God and all that God created. As Francis Schaeffer has pointed out, this dominion is proof of moral responsibility: They were not to assume that whatever is, is right. They were to govern the world according to God's principles.

Birds, fish, and creeping things—all these were under man's authority. The serpent who showed up uninvited in their garden and now spoke to them so compassionately—this beast was subject to Adam's command. If the birds and fish were under Adam's domain, the serpent most assuredly would have left with but a single word from Adam's lips.

Incredibly, Adam was seduced by a creature who was beneath him. He withdrew from his God-given responsibility and accepted the word of a beast. Man, who could have walked tall among the creatures, now stoops to the suggestion of one of them.

Adam dropped the scepter and Satan picked it up. Man, created to be king of the earth, would now become a slave and be everywhere in chains.

- He sows but does not know whether he will reap.
- He builds but does not know whether the work of his hands will be destroyed by tornadoes, hurricanes, or earthquakes.
- He enjoys his sexual freedom and ends up with broken relationships, betrayal, and sexually transmitted diseases.
- He solves one medical mystery only to be haunted by another.
- He establishes friendships only to be overcome by jealousy, mistrust, and hatred.
- Finally, he is a slave to death. No matter how many insurance programs he has, no matter how good his doctors, in the end, death will claim its victim.

Adam and Eve, like the dog in Aesop's fable who dropped its bone to snatch at a reflection in the water, discovered that they had traded fellowship with God for a mirage. The promise of Satan was not only hollow, but laced with poison. But there was no turning back.

In Eden, the crown slid from man's head. Satan picked it up from the dust and crowned himself—but the victory was tarnished. Barnhouse wrote:

He grasped the sword of power with both hands, but he took it by the blade and so wounded himself on its sharp edges that he could not with his hands take up his food and henceforth lapped it from the earth, and dust has been the flavor of all that he ever tasted.[2]

He would now treat the world as if it belonged to him. He

was successful in separating man from God, but there was yet more work to be done. He wanted man's allegiance and worship.

GOD'S RESPONSE

God was prepared for this hour, and He kept His promise.

Adam and Eve Were Judged

On the day they ate, they died. Death is both a process and a crisis. As a process, death began the moment Adam and Eve ate the fruit. When this process was complete, it would end in a crisis. Their souls would be separated from their bodies.

But something worse happened. Man's soul was also separated from God. Adam and Eve and their descendants lost their reference point. Just as surely as a light is unplugged from its socket, Adam and Eve woke to find a barrier of shame between them and God.

They now "knew good and evil" by an unsettled, awakened conscience. Separated from God, they became separated from one another. They covered themselves with fig leaves to hide from each other and from God. They even felt an internal separation, the soul separated from itself. They would live as restless creatures in a turbulent world.

The Serpent Was Judged

"Because you have done this, cursed are you more than all cattle, and more than every beast of the field; on your belly shall you go, and dust shall you eat all the days of your life" (Genesis 3:14). Perhaps it is not without symbolic significance that the serpent, I am told, is the only animal that cannot move backwards. Now that the decision was made, the serpent of Paradise found himself in an ally, able only to plunge ahead from one blunder to another.

God promises that He will "put enmity" between the serpent and the woman and that the seed of the woman will crush the serpent's head. In the next chapter we shall look more closely at this promise of a coming redeemer. For now, we need simply remind ourselves that God was prepared for the mess Adam and

Eve had made. Though Adam and Eve ate voluntarily, they were doing what God knew would happen; even better, they did what God was prepared to have happen.

God's Eternal Plan Was Revealed

If someone were to hold your head six inches from the wing of a jet plane, you would have no idea what you were looking at. The markings in the shiny metal would hardly look artistic; the length and breadth of the structure would be unknown to you. As for its purpose, you could only guess what this small slice of hard surface would represent. But if your perspective was broadened, you could make more sense out of the details.

Only because God invites us to stand back and see His plan from the standpoint of eternity does the mystery of Satan and evil make any sense. Of course we do not see everything, but we are given a glimpse into the distant past. What we discover is that before anything was created, God already had a blueprint; the fall of Lucifer (and subsequent fall of man) was already included in the grand design. Paul wrote to Titus, "For the faith of those chosen of God and the knowledge of the truth which is according to godliness, in hope of eternal life, which God, who cannot lie, promised in the ages long ago" (Titus 1:1–2).

God made a promise in "ages long ago." That does not refer to the ages since creation, but in eternity past. Paul wrote to Timothy that God saved us "according to His own purpose and grace which was granted us in Christ Jesus *from all eternity*" (2 Timothy 1:9, italics added). Indeed, the author of Hebrews says that we are saved through the "blood of the eternal covenant" (Hebrews 13:20).

Obviously, God's covenant, made in the distant ages of eternity, could not have been made with angels or men. The agreement was made between the members of the Trinity. God the Father, who loves His Son perfectly, promised Him a gift of redeemed humanity as a special expression of love. Already, even so far back, the fall of man and his subsequent redemption was not only foreknown but a part of the grand plan. Little wonder Christ always referred to these people as those whom the Father "has given Me" (John 6:37; 10:29; 17:9). Christ said that the Father loves us even as He loves the Son, and the Son was loved "before the foundation of the world" (John 17:23–24). Yes, we were loved long before the serpent deceived our first parents with his lies!

John, speaking of those who will remain steadfast in persecution, wrote, "And all who dwell on the earth will worship him, everyone whose name has not been written from the foundation of the world in the book of life of the Lamb who has been slain" (Revelation 13:8). The Book of Life was not created because God had to change his plans when Adam and Eve sinned. Those who would be redeemed were *already* written in the Book of Life before Eve ever touched the beautiful fruit of Eden.

This is not the place to try to explain all of the questions we have about what God did and why He did it. Struggle as we might with the mysteries of God's plan, we can simply rejoice in Paul's words: "Just as He chose us in Him before the foundation of the world, that we would be holy and blameless before him" (Ephesians 1:4). There is little use trying to explain this text by resorting to fanciful ideas about how for God eternity past is actually now. We should simply take delight in the fact that God did the choosing, and that He did it before the world was created.

There were no emergency counsels in heaven when Adam and Eve sinned. There was no need to cancel other plans, no desperate attempt to counter the work of the evil fiend, no need to devise a strategy that was not already meticulously in place. God's plan encompasses everything. "For by Him all things were created, both in the heavens and on earth, visible and invisible, whether thrones or dominions or rulers or authorities—all things have been created through Him and for Him" (Colossians 1:16).

The creation of heaven and earth—*through* Him and *for* Him. Visible and invisible entities—*through* Him and *for* Him. Kingdoms and authorities—*through* Him and *for* Him. Angels, good and evil—*through* Him and *for* Him.

The fall of man would culminate in greater worship, greater appreciation, and greater display of God's mighty attributes. The grace of God and His justice and love would now be put on display. As for Lucifer, turned Satan, he would continue to exist for the glory of God just as he had done in ages past. His motives would be different and God would treat him as an enemy and not a friend, but he would end up following God's decree.

Satan left the Garden of Eden with only half of his objective accomplished. He had succeeded in getting man to be separated from God, but there was much more to do. He was not content with a man who would go his own way; he wanted a man who would follow the serpent's way. Detached from God, but attached to the Serpent—that was what the Evil One desired.

In order to lure man away from God, the serpent planted the seeds of occult religion, hoping to hide behind those trappings to receive worship. His greatest desire was to duplicate religious experience, hoping that man would have contact with him but think he was in contact with God.

The five lies in Eden form the heart of all occult religion, whether in ancient Babylon or modern America. When the Serpent speaks, at least some people listen.

Keep reading.

4

THE SERPENT'S NEW RELIGION

For a moment let's try to enter the mind of Satan.

What if you had a hateful passion to deceive everyone who inhabits planet earth? What if you had the ability to inject thoughts into the minds of some people which they think are their own? You are consumed with a desire to be worshiped. But you can't reveal your evil nature to the human race and expect to be accepted. So you set up a rival religion that makes sense to man, but you control it backstage. Your goal is to convince humans that they are experiencing God, when in point of fact they are actually in contact with you. Being worshiped under a disguise is better than not being worshiped at all.

And so it was that in the Garden of Eden the roots of occult religion began. Satan did not try to disprove the existence of God in his temptation of Adam and Eve. His goal was not to make Adam and Eve atheists; rather, his goal was to persuade them to worship another god. To put it briefly, Satan was competing with God for the allegiance of men.

THE FIVE LIES OF OCCULTISM

Occultism has many forms, but it usually has five major

premises. Whether the religions of the East or the flowering of contemporary New Age thought, all are fruits that have blossomed from the seeds planted in Eden. On that fateful day, Satan revealed the lies by which he would attempt to deceive the world.

You will recognize them easily.

The Lie of Reincarnation

God had said that in the day that Adam and Eve ate from the forbidden tree, they would "surely die" (Genesis 2:17). And as we have already pointed out, though their bodies continued to function, the process of death had begun. They were destined for the grave. Not surprisingly, God was right.

To counter God's clear warning that Adam and Eve were to die if they ate of the tree, Satan offered a promise of his own: "You surely shall not die!" (3:4). It was a blatant contradiction of what the Almighty had just said.

Was the serpent's lie believable? I don't think so, and Satan knew it. Adam and Eve died, and so have all subsequent generations. The cemeteries throughout the world are proof that Satan was lying. Death is all around us; we all fear it. Even atheists dread the moment.

But with some ingenuity and deceit, this lie has been passed off to millions of people. The lie has been remade, reinterpreted as the doctrine of reincarnation. Yes, your present body will die, the spiel goes, but you go on living in another body somewhere on the earth. You go round and round, getting as many chances as you need in your quest for perfection. You take with you the wisdom you accumulated in this life and use it in the next. There is no judgment; therefore, death is not to be feared.

Reincarnation teaches that souls play a kind of musical chairs with the various bodies in the world. In this life you are one person, but in the next life you are someone else. Ever onward and upward, the process moves relentlessly forward as we better ourselves in each cycle. A New Age couple who kissed each other before they jumped off the Golden Gate Bridge left a note in the car in which the man wrote, "I love you all; I wish I could stay, but I must hurry. The suspense is killing me."

Reincarnation is based on the cruel doctrine of karma, an impersonal, irrevocable law that says that everyone gets what he or she deserves. Evil is always punished in the life to come; good is always rewarded. That means that people begin their earthly lives at different levels. Some people, because of sin, have forfeited all privileges. Others, because of good works, have been born into high positions and are well on their way to nirvana. The best example of this is seen in Hinduism, where everyone is rigidly divided into five levels: four castes followed by the outcasts, those who do not even merit a caste. The basic principle is that the poor exist to serve the rich.

Karma teaches that there is no injustice in the world. Everything that happens occurs because of some previous good or evil. Consider the cruelty of this doctrine. Imagine saying to an abused child, "You are actually getting what you deserve because of sins committed in a previous existence."

His most dazzling deception: a counterfeit religious experience.

Shirley MacLaine, an actress who has popularized New Age teaching, says confidently that death does not exist. She "discovered" that in previous lives she was a princess in Atlantis, an Inca in Peru, and even a child raised by elephants.

In this philosophy death is not to be feared, for as traditionally understood, it does not occur. There is no personal God to whom we must give an account. You can continue to live the way you are, believing for the most part whatever you wish. To quote Shirley MacLaine, it is like shooting a movie: "You just keep doing it until you get it right."

Reincarnation is the devil's lie made believable; it is a clever deception remade for popular consumption. Evidence for reincarnation is not based on the transmigration of souls, but on the transmigration of demons. Those who are in contact with evil spirits often have knowledge of previous times and places.

Nevertheless, today there are many who are deceived and agree with the devil: We do *not* surely die!

The Lie of Esotericism

Now that Satan had neatly set aside God's Word as a basis for truth, what would serve as a substitute? He promised Eve that her "eyes would be opened" (Genesis 3:5). She would have an experience of enlightenment resulting in a perception of reality that would give her mystical insight.

Satan's ultimate desire is not for men and women to commit immorality or even look to astrology for guidance or to be healed by crystals. All those are stepping-stones to his most dazzling deception: a counterfeit religious experience. He wants humans to encounter him and think they are in touch with the true God. This experience of enlightenment is a "satanic conversion."

This philosophy is esotericism, the belief in a transformation of consciousness that initiates us into true spirituality. New Age literature is filled with references to "light" or "enlightenment." In pagan Greece and Rome, this enlightenment was based on a theory of secret knowledge that could be obtained by searching the depths of one's own soul. In reality it involves an encounter with a spiritual being.

Many years ago, Marilyn Ferguson wrote in *The Aquarian Conspiracy* that an "irrevocable shift" is overtaking us. It is not a new system but a new mind. Society is being changed on an "enlarged concept of human potential . . . a transformation of personal consciousness."[1]

There are two popular doorways through which evil spirits are able to bring about this counterfeit "new birth" experience. One is transcendental meditation, which aims to empty the mind of all conscious thought. This kind of meditation is designed to unite the soul with the one unified force of the universe.

As long as I am thinking about something, I perceive myself to be distinct from the objects of this world. So the occultists tell us that we must have an experience in which such distinctions disappear and we lose ourselves in the vast ocean of impersonal energy. Normal reasoning must be suspended. The will must be surrendered to the god-force of the universe.

Popular New Age teaching is that we can be in contact with

"masters of wisdom" who can share their insights and energy with us. We can be in touch with "the powers" and discover that there are gods all around us who are only too eager to help us in our quest for being united with the divine. These entities help us in our own transformation.

We must bear in mind that the earth is populated with evil spirits who followed Lucifer in his rebellion who are only too eager to give such clients a religious experience. Contact with these powers results in so-called enlightenment. Just as Satan promised Adam and Eve, they are to have a transformation of consciousness that will make them god-like.

The second doorway for spirits to enter is through psychedelic drugs. Marilyn Ferguson says that the psychedelic experience is a faster route to a new perception of reality. Annette Hollander, in *How to Help Your Child Have a Spiritual Life,* gives an account of people who have had mystical encounters while on drugs.[2]

Many people falsely assume that demons communicate only evil ideas, not realizing that these spirits might often give good advice and mouth sound doctrine. When our Lord was here on earth, demons confessed that He was the Christ.

Demons are liars who receive perverted satisfaction in deceiving gullible humans. Should the truth serve their purposes, they will use it; when half-truths are called for, they have them in their arsenal; but lying is their most popular weapon. I believe demons are assigned to a given individual; and because they study the history and behavior of their subject, they become very knowledgeable regarding that person's past. After the person has died, these spirits are open to the possibility of communicating with relatives and friends who want to have a conversation with their departed loved one. A channeler is contacted who purports to "call up" the dead and establish communication. But in fact, the communication is not with the dead, but with a demon who was acquainted with the dead. Hence the Bible calls them "familiar spirits."

C. S. Lewis perceptively realized that the highest form of deception would be for demons to duplicate religious experiences. The fictional demon Screwtape, in giving instructions to his underling Wormwood, says, "I have great hopes that we shall learn in due time how to emotionalize and mythologize their science to such an extent that what is, in effect, a belief in us (though not under that name) will creep in while the human mind remains closed to belief in the Enemy [God]."[3]

And so it is that throughout the centuries the lie of Eden has taken hold. Millions claim to have had an "opening of the eyes," the experience of enlightenment. They claim to belong to the initiated who understand one another because they belong to the inner circle.

The seeds of Eden have borne bitter fruit.

The Lie of Pantheism

The heart of the serpent's deception lies in these words, "You will be like God" (Genesis 3:5). The phrase is not, "You shall be like gods" (as in the King James Version), but rather, "You shall be as God" (Elohim).

To be like God is an awesome thought. Man is intelligent enough to know that he is not the creator of the planets, stars, and trees. So this is another lie that had to be adapted for public consumption.

There was only one way that this lie could survive, and that is by extending the idea of divinity to include everything that exists. The reasoning goes like this, "Yes, I am God, but so is nature . . . in fact, *everything* is God."

Pantheism is the conception of God that pervades all occult religion. The prefix *pan* means "all" and refers to the idea that all that exists is God; there are many different levels of existence that correspond to different levels of divinity. Pantheism is most easily remembered as the view that "God is all and all is God."

For the pantheist, the final reality in the universe is spiritual; in fact, matter is illusory. We must deny the existence of the material universe to escape into the world of the mind, which is in touch with the spiritual universe that is truly real.

One implication of pantheism is that man is his own savior. Whereas Christianity teaches that man fell into sin and needs to be rescued by Christ, pantheism teaches that man didn't really fall, but God did! What happened was this: At one time matter and mind were united as one; they were one continuous, unified force called God. But matter and mind separated, and this breach must be healed by us. Salvation means that matter and mind are reunited through meditation.

Think through the words of Nikos Kazantzakis, the author of *The Last Temptation of Christ* (the book on which the controversial movie was based). "It is not God who will save us—it is we who will save God, by battling, by creating, and transmuting matter into spirit."[4]

Atonement is defined to mean "at-one-ment" with the original creation. The possibility of salvation thus rests wholly with us. We redeem God by bringing our "fallen god" of matter and spirit back together.

Pantheism, I might add, devalues human life. If I were to say that you are God, you might consider it a compliment, but such a statement is not a compliment if the same can be said of worms and thistles!

Several years ago, on a TV miniseries, Shirley MacLaine ran onto Malibu beach shouting, "I'm God! I'm God!" She echoed the words of many who claim that this is the most important revelation to be passed on to the peoples of the world.

The deity of man is a lie that will be widely believed at the end of the age. In fact, Paul says that when the Antichrist comes, he will work in accord with Satan. He will claim to be God, and the world will believe him because "God will send upon them a deluding influence so that they will believe what is false" (2 Thessalonians 2:11).

Multitudes will worship the Antichrist because they will believe he is God. And if we are all gods already, why cannot this special man be thought of as the supreme manifestation of God?

And so the lie of Eden is heard around the world, "Ye shall be like God."

The Lie of Relativism

"You will be like God, knowing good and evil" (Genesis 3:5).

Satan promised Adam and Eve an experiential knowledge of "good and evil." With this experience, man, now left to himself, would be able to distinguish good and evil on his own—or so the serpent implied. Since man is his own god, he is free to write his own rules.

We have already learned that the serpent was quite right in this respect: Disobedience did give Adam and Eve a new knowledge of evil. They did not merely know evil abstractly as a concept of the mind, but as the probing of a restless conscience. From that point on, their moral perception was clouded as they struggled with the need to reconcile their lifestyle with the image of God, which had been defaced but not erased from their minds and hearts.

The problem, of course, is that in their fallen state they could never again perceive good and evil as God saw it. If left to themselves, they would have to build their own system of conduct with the fragmentary knowledge of their own sinful perceptions and tainted conscience. What is more, they would discover that they could not live up to what they intuitively knew to be right. Simply put, they would have to become relativists, giving up all hope of finding a unified system of morality and truth.

Relativism is the word we use to describe the popular belief that "what is true for me might not be true for you." The philosopher and educator John Dewey is credited with giving relativism respectability in America. He believed that morality, like language, varied from culture to culture, and that, therefore, no one moral belief was superior to another.

Relativism thrives in our culture. While watching an interview on television, I heard a woman admitting that she was having an affair with another woman's husband. Sensing that this still might be considered improper to some members of the listening audience, she felt constrained to add, "Of course, what I am doing may not be right for everyone, but it's what is best for me."

Eastern religions believe in relativism for diverse reasons. If it is true that God is everything, it follows that God is also evil. That is why Hinduism teaches that good and evil are only illusions and only appear to differ from one another. Allan Watts, who is credited with making Zen Buddhism palatable to Americans, explains it this way: Life is like a play where you see good and bad men in conflict on the stage, but behind the curtain, they are the best of friends. Backstage God and Satan go hand in hand.

To quote Yen-Men, one of the great Eastern teachers, "If you wish the plain truth, be not concerned about right and wrong. The conflict between right and wrong is the sickness of the mind."[5]

Since evil does not exist, it follows that man's problem is not sin but ignorance. All that we need is enlightenment. The result is that I never have to feel guilty about how I treat you. Even betrayal, theft, or personal injury need not fill me with regret. To cling to an objective standard of conduct is archaic and unnecessary for the simple reason that such a standard does not exist.

Whether relativism comes clothed in Western culture or in the admittedly irrational views of the East, the result is the same. Without an objective standard of morality, the most hideous crimes can be justified. What is more, no one lives consistently with the relativism that he espouses. If you steal a relativist's car or rape his wife, he immediately appeals to an objective standard of morality!

Relativism is also contrary to the conscience that still resides in us as fallen beings, however imperfect it might be. We know that there are some things that are always evil, no matter the circumstances or the culture. Our problem is that, left to ourselves, we cannot defend our beliefs rationally. So each person becomes a law unto himself.

Yes, Adam and Eve came to "know good and evil." But this "knowledge" was a curse and not a blessing. Man was to spend much energy trying to appease his conscience and cope with the guilt of breaking a standard he intuitively knew was right. For the most part, he would try to erase the boundaries and do as he pleases.

There is one more lie that rules much of the world.

The Lie of Hedonism

What motivated Eve to disobey God? True, she was deceived, thinking that the serpent was clarifying God's instructions. But she also was misled because of her fascination with the forbidden fruit.

When the woman saw that the tree was good for food, and that it was a delight to the eyes, and that the tree was desirable to make one wise, she took from its fruit and ate; and she gave also to her husband with her, and he ate. (Genesis 3:6)

Eve's intuition told her, "Feel, don't think!" Objective truth is too cold, too harsh; the words of God are not as important as the right sensation. Since the world cannot be comprehended rationally, and since the knowledge you have does not entirely satisfy, go with your feelings.

And so our world accepts the philosophy of Woody Allen: "The heart wants what it wants!" What you believe is not important; you must simply go with your heart. Thus men leave their wives to find happiness with other women; women leave their husbands to find their dream. Since you only "go around" once in life, you have to "grab for the gusto," as the advertisement suggests. Little wonder everyone does "what is right in his own eyes."

Although the word *hedonism* is often associated with a commitment to sexual pleasure however obtained, it has a broader application in our society. The doctrine that pleasure or one's happiness is the highest good has been the spark that has ignited many an evil deed.

We cannot put Humpty Dumpty back together again.

Philosophers have tried to curb hedonism by saying that we should act in ways that maximize not only our own happiness, but also the happiness of the greatest number. This rationalization has only justified the grossest evil. If Hitler believed that 6 million Jews stood in the path of the happiness of 90 million Germans, he had an obligation to secure the happiness of the greatest number. What lies!

GOD, THE SERPENT, AND YOU

When Satan saw Eve eat of the tree and give to Adam who was standing with her, he was elated. Any misgivings he had about his decision to rebel against God were for the moment forgotten. He had succeeded in separating man from God; now it appeared that man would attach himself to Satan. As far as Satan knew, the entire human race would now side with him in his rebellion against God. If he could not have all of the angels, at least he could have all of this new breed of creatures called humans. He was quite confident, and quite right, that the sin of Adam and Eve would contaminate their descendants.

When God came walking in the cool of the day, Adam and Eve did not run to meet Him but hid among the trees, covering themselves with fig leaves. The switch had been pulled. Darkness settled upon their consciences, and they were helpless in making it right.

In Philadelphia, I'm told, some graffiti was scrawled on a wall that read, "Humpty Dumpty was pushed!!" A reminder that the mess we make is always the fault of someone else! When God asked Adam if he had eaten of the tree, Adam refused to answer and blamed it on his wife. "The woman whom You gave to be with me, she gave me from the tree and I ate," he said (Genesis 3:12). The fault, Adam says, lies with the weak-willed woman God created for him. Please notice that he shifted the blame to her, though there wasn't the slightest chance that he had married the wrong woman!

Adam and Eve, like Lucifer before them, learned that we might be able to push Humpty Dumpty from the shelf, but we cannot put him back together again. Only God can restore the beauty of a marred creation. Or, to put it in Humpty Dumpty language, though a man can choose to break an egg, no series of choices can ever put it back together!

As for God, He would not be mocked. He had words for the Serpent. "I will put enmity between you and the woman, and between your seed and her seed; he shall bruise you on the head, and you shall bruise him on the heel" (Genesis 3:15).

Here we have the first statement of the gospel in the Old Testament. God would become involved in the conflict. Regardless of how sturdy the tree of false religion would become, eventually it would be chopped down. The conflict would be intense, but in the end God would win. God would do what Adam and Eve could not. Several more points need to be made about God's response to the situation now presented in the Garden of Eden.

1. *God takes the initiative in the battle.* He says, "I will." Lucifer had said "I will," and now God says, "I will." Two wills would be in conflict in an attempt to rule the world. Even before man could look to God for help, God already promised it. If there was a mess to be cleaned up, God would do it. He would put the broken egg back together.

2. *The Serpent would be crushed by a mediator.* If it was the woman who was deceived by the serpent, it was now the woman whose seed would crush the evil creature. She would have a male child who would strike the fatal blow. Of her seed, God says, "He shall bruise you on the head" (v. 15).

3. *This victory would be accomplished through suffering.* There would be deliverance for mankind, but it would not be an easy deliverance. This "enmity" would result in a contrast of wounds. The seed of the woman would crush the Serpent's head; in return, the Serpent would only be able to nip the Redeemer's heel (v. 15). The difference would be like that between a knock-out punch and a slap on the wrist.

Satan could not foresee this divine intervention. He did not know that God would take the initiative and reconcile humans to Himself. He did not know that this would be his own doom and downfall. The conflict that he thought he could control was taken out of his hands. *The battle would no longer be between the Serpent and man, but more ominously, between the Serpent and God.*

The greater the lies, the greater the punishment. The Serpent will be judged not only for his initial act of rebellion but for all of the subsequent disobedience that flowed from it. Of necessity he loses whenever he wins. No matter how much havoc he creates now, God has all of eternity to set the record straight. And He will.

The paint was splattered over the canvas, but God was about to use the mess to create his own picture. The Serpent saw only today; tomorrow was hidden from his sight. God viewed the picture quite differently: This was just the fulfillment of the promise of eternal life made in the ages long ago.

The Serpent did not know that someday there would be a man named John Newton who would be so vile that he would challenge his friends to think of some sin that he had not yet committed. Yet, he would eventually be redeemed by God and write:

> Amazing Grace! how sweet the sound,
> That saved a wretch like me!
> I once was lost, but now am found,
> Was blind, but now I see.

When we've been there ten thousand years,
Bright shining as the sun,
We've no less days to sing God's praise
Than when we first begun.

Despite hearing God's promise, the Serpent did not concede defeat. Though he had been told that he would be crushed, he chose to play out the rest of the game even though each day the stakes would rise still higher and his subsequent plunge would become much deeper.

He would strike back with the vain hope that God's plan might yet be thwarted. Indeed, there were some moments when it looked as if he might win. So he chose illusion over reality. Better a vain hope than none at all.

And now the conflict begins to heat up.

5

THE SERPENT
STRIKES BACK

There is a story, perhaps apocryphal, of a construction company that invited various contractors to submit bids for a major building complex. All things being equal, the contractor who submitted the lowest bid would get the job. Needless to say, the bids had to be submitted in secret.

On the last day that bids could be tendered, a contractor walked into the office of the president of the company with a bid application in his hand. To his surprise, the office was empty; he stood alone, venturing a glance at the huge mahogany desk.

Much to his surprise, he saw the bid of his major competitor lying open on the desk. The only problem was that there was a can of soda sitting directly over the most important figure in the document. If this contractor knew the amount that was written on that line, he could adjust his own bid to come in just beneath it and the multimillion dollar job would be his.

The contractor nervously paced the floor, knowing full well what was at stake. He contemplated moving the can for just a second, reading the figure, and then putting it down. He touched the can but found himself unable to do it.

He glanced around the room one more time. Now, confident that no one was looking, he lifted the can quickly, intending to glance at the number and then put the can back instantly. Much to his chagrin, as he lifted the can from the desk hundreds of BBs spilled onto the desk and rolled onto the floor.

That contractor experienced the law of unintended consequences firsthand. He thought he could control the fallout of his dishonesty but discovered that unforeseen events had been built into the temptation. One single act had repercussions he could not have anticipated. The can of soda was not what it appeared to be.

If not innocently, at least naively, Adam and Eve disobeyed God, without realizing that they were setting in motion a moral and spiritual earthquake that would reverberate throughout the universe. They, like Lucifer before them, had no idea of the moral and spiritual aftershocks their single act of disobedience might generate. They must have been surprised that one small evil produced an endless chain of larger ones.

We have learned already that angels were created individually and fell individually; they have no mother or father. There is no difficulty in believing that only a third fell and the other two-thirds retained their loyalty to Jehovah. But in the case of man, the entire race was to descend from Adam and Eve; thus, when they sinned, they took all of their descendants with them. From that point on, every human being would be tainted with the sin virus.

When Satan learned that he would be crushed by the "seed of the woman," that is, someone who would be born through the birth process, he tried to identify his protagonists and fight against them. He tried to kill anyone who looked like he might be the promised redeemer. The destruction of the royal seed would now be his highest priority. The history of this conflict dominates much of the Old Testament.

The serpent strikes wherever he can with his deadly poison. Though he knows his doom is sure, he fights as if he has a chance. Just the thought of victory must satisfy him. He must be content with the knowledge that he would nip the heel of the woman's seed. If he celebrates, it is always too soon.

Time and again God allowed Satan to make what might appear to be a fatal blow against the plan of God only to discover that he had been outwitted. No matter how close the contest seems to be, God always has the last move on the chessboard.

The serpent will make a series of strikes against God and His people. But God holds the trump card.

A STRIKE AGAINST THE FAMILY: DIVIDE THEM

Adam and Eve had a firstborn son who filled their lives with hope. They named him Cain, which means "the gotten one." Little did they know that this gift of God would dash their dreams to the ground. They were the first parents to be disappointed by the life of a child, but not the last. Throughout history many parents would face the challenge of "raising Cain"!

Cain seems to have been a contented child until his brother Abel was born. Then there was sibling rivalry, a rivalry that would end in murder. The conflict was over false religion and true. God accepted Abel's offering, taken from among the flocks; He rejected Cain's offering, which was the fruit of the ground. Perhaps the difference lay in the character of the offering. An offering of blood was accepted, whereas the offering from the fruit of the ground was rejected. If this is so, then Cain and Abel must have received explicit instructions from God about the kind of offering that was required. Perhaps they did, but we don't know for sure.

Another explanation, perhaps correct, is that the content of the offering was not important; it was the faith by which it was offered that made the difference. In Hebrews 11:4 we read, "By faith Abel offered to God a better sacrifice than Cain, through which he obtained testimony that he was righteous, God testifying about his gifts, and through faith, though he is dead, he still speaks." Whether it was the content of the sacrifice or simply the attitude with which it was offered, we do know that Cain thought he could come to God on his own terms, in his own way, and without a change of heart.

This strong-willed firstborn resented his brother. He felt the bitter sting of rejection, the feeling that he was not as presentable as his younger sibling. If he had lived in our day, a psychiatrist would have diagnosed him as having low self-esteem, the cure for which was to see himself as valuable. He would just have to accept himself, to love himself as he was. After all, he was inherently valuable, just as worthy as his brother.

Or was he?

Today counseling has become a popular vocation. We all believe people need good advice, administered with heavy doses of love and unconditional self-acceptance. But God did not speak to Cain about such matters. He told him plainly that he could expect God's approval only if he had a change of heart: "Why are you angry? And why has your countenance fallen? If you do well, will not your countenance be lifted up? And if you do not do well, sin is crouching at the door; and its desire is for you, but you must master it" (Genesis 4:6–7). If Cain would please God by doing right, all would be well. But if not, sin was crouching like a ferocious beast at the door ready to pounce on him. *Either he would master sin, or sin would master him.*

God would deliver some from under his grasp.

Cain was not a good counselee. He did not do his prescribed homework. He chose to nurture his jealousy rather than confess it and find mercy. Rather than repent and commit the matter into God's hands, his evil heart contemplated a sinister means of evening the score. He could appease his vengeance by killing his brother. With him out of the way, he could achieve the self-satisfaction he craved and be true to his own desires.

The jealousy flamed into anger. Cain attacked Abel, and for the first time in history, human blood was spilled on the ground. Was this just normal sibling rivalry gone amiss? Yes, and a whole lot more. Satan was fanning Cain's anger. We read that Cain slew Abel because he was "of the evil one" (1 John 3:10–12). Cain had opened his life to an unseen enemy. Yes, he was responsible for what he had done, for he—not Satan—committed the ghastly deed. But when Satan encouraged Cain's jealousy to fester, he was joining with Cain in carrying out the first murder in cold blood.

The anger of Satan was understandable, if not rational. After Adam and Eve ate the forbidden fruit, he thought that the whole human race would now be on his side. It made him very angry to discover that God would deliver some from under his grasp. To ease that anger, he would attack righteous people like Abel and treat any godly human being as a threat.

Satan almost certainly saw Abel as "the seed" of the "woman" (Genesis 3:15). He thought that the prophecy God had made in the Garden of Eden was being fulfilled before his eyes. He had thought that he had turned this prophecy on its head; with Abel lying on the ground drenched in his own blood, Satan believed that he had now crushed the head of God's redeemer. Perhaps he had turned the tables and had delivered the crushing blow. Swirling in Satan's mind was the headline: "Satan Outwits God."

Or had he? God now gave Adam and Eve another son whose name was Seth, meaning "substitute." Satan then understood that no matter how many murders he instigated, no matter how many descendants he destroyed, others would always rise up and take their place. Thwarting the plans of God would be more difficult than he had supposed.

The discord within the first family mirrored the division of the whole human race. There would always be the battle between the righteous and the unrighteous. Cain was the first, but not the last devotee of false religion. Centuries later, a New Testament writer would describe arrogant religious teachers as those who "revile the things which they do not understand; and the things which they know by instinct, like unreasoning animals, by these things they are destroyed. Woe to them! For they have gone the way of Cain, and for pay they have rushed headlong into the error of Balaam, and perished in the rebellion of Korah" (Jude 10–11).

"The way of Cain" is the way of arrogant, false religion. He was the prototype of those who seek acceptance on their own terms, not God's. The person you meet on the plane today, or the neighbor who lives next door who believes that we can choose our own way to God, can trace his spiritual lineage to Cain.

What happened when God confronted Cain with his sin? Like his father Adam, he tried to shift blame, evading questions and feigning ignorance. "Where is Abel your brother?" the Lord asked (Genesis 4:9). To which Cain replied, "I do not know. Am I my brother's keeper?" Cain is lying, of course. There is no truth in him.

God puts a curse on Cain. "Now you are cursed from the ground, which has opened its mouth to receive your brother's blood from your hand" (v. 11). Cain complained that his punishment was too great and out of proportion to the crime committed. So God put a mark on him to forbid anyone from killing him, and Cain was condemned to a life of ceaseless wandering. Cain went out to form a godless society and settled in the land of Nod (lit. "wandering"), east of Eden (v. 16).

The sweetness of revenge was not worth the suffering he later experienced. He chose his own path, thinking that if he put himself first, that would be best for him. He did not learn a lesson all of us should remember: *The will of God is something all of us would choose if we had all the facts.*

Cain married either a sister or cousin and fathered a child, Enoch, and named a city after him. This civilization for the most part follows in the footsteps of its progenitor. Cain begets descendants in his own arrogant likeness. This society which abandons God nevertheless prospers. It produces music, weapons, agricultural devices, cities, and culture. And with an increase in wisdom comes an increase in wickedness.

The Serpent's first attack was against a family and was an attempt to kill a righteous man. The attack was the expression of a religious conflict between two brothers, one of whom could not be content to see the other prosper. Behind the human dynamics was the struggle between God and Satan, between the seed of the woman and the seed of the Serpent.

Today, Satan has given up on trying to destroy the seed of the woman, for Christ has already come. But he continues his attack against our families. That is his primary means of "getting back at God."

God designed the family to propagate the faith from one generation to another. Fathers are to teach their children about God; the children are to teach their children. Today we are plagued with dysfunctional homes, abuse, immorality, and addictions— all of these are a part of the serpent's plan to destroy God's witness in the world.

The Serpent's poison spills beyond our homes into our churches, offices, and factories. It spills over into society and government. This poison has instigated many a war and has claimed millions of casualties. The history of the human race is the record of fallen humanity stumbling along, choosing the way of Cain rather than the way of Abel.

What about the descendants of Seth, the replacement of Abel? They began to make proclamations in the name of the Lord. From Seth will come Noah and Abraham, people who seek God and receive His blessing. Eventually, the seed of the woman will appear.

The Serpent's first retaliatory strike had done its work. Though it might appear that God was keeping His distance, in reality His agenda was on schedule. Much to the serpent's dismay, a seed was being preserved and at least a few men and women were calling on the name of the Lord.

God proved that, though members of the race might be killed, He could raise up others to inherit the promise. The victories of the Serpent would eventually be shown to be illusory.

A STRIKE AGAINST SOCIETY: CORRUPT THEM

If the Serpent could not kill the promised seed, his second strategy was to corrupt it. As humans began to multiply upon the earth, wickedness began to increase. The wickedness was so great that "every intent of the thoughts of his heart was only evil continually" (Genesis 6:5).

Genesis 6 has provoked controversy, and with good reason. We read, "Now it came about, when men began to multiply on the face of the land, and daughters were born to them, that the sons of God saw that the daughters of men were beautiful; and they took wives for themselves, whomever they chose" (6:1–2). "Sons of God" intermarrying with "daughters of men"?

That phrase "sons of God" has been interpreted in two ways. Some think it refers simply to the godly line of Seth, whereas the "daughters of men" were the Canaanites, or the descendants of Cain. In other words, the phrase would describe the intermarriage of a righteous race with an unrighteous one. But that does not do justice to the terminology and the context.

Others think that these "sons of God" were demons who cohabited with women on this earth. We know that there are verified accounts of fallen angels who have assumed human form and had sexual intercourse, but it is unlikely that such a union could cause conception. Though fallen angels can assume human form, so far as we know, they cannot beget life.

A better way to understand this passage is to take the phrase "sons of God" as a description of powerful rulers who were controlled (indwelt) by fallen angels. These evil angels left their abode and inhabited bodies of human warriors, the mighty ones of the earth. These mighty rulers were not divine, nor were they the offspring of the gods (as often believed in pagan religions).

Instead, these "mighty men, who were men of renown," were ordinary human beings given superhuman strength because they were demonically controlled. They lived lives of rampant sexuality and violence. They married as many women as they wished and engaged in all manner of sexual perversion. The children of these marriages were not god-kings, but men of flesh and blood who eventually died in the flood.

God was watching. "Then the Lord saw that the wickedness of man was great on the earth, and that every intent of the thoughts of his heart was only evil continually" (v. 5). God was sorry that He had made man; that is, God was grieved at their wickedness and decided that He would, in effect, give the race a new beginning. A flood would destroy all the inhabitants of the world.

Most probably, the Serpent's hope revived. If all of mankind was drowned, the seed of the woman would be obliterated. What the serpent could not do, God, apparently, was doing Himself. The Almighty would send a flood and an entire civilization would be blotted out.

But again God snatched victory from the jaws of defeat. "But Noah found favor in the eyes of the Lord" (v. 8). A family would be spared and through them the seed of the woman would yet come. The serpent, though gratified at the thought of the untimely death of the wicked, still had more work to do.

As for those evil spirits who inhabited the ancient rulers, God confined them to a gloomy dungeon, and I believe they are no longer free to roam the earth. Peter wrote, "For if God did not spare angels when they sinned, but cast them into hell [Tartarus] and committed them to pits of darkness, reserved for judgment; and did not spare the ancient world, but preserved Noah, a preacher of righteousness" (2 Peter 2:4–5). There is a group of angels who are already under direct judgment, but not yet cast into the lake of fire.

These spirits were confined just before the days of Noah; they were participants in the worldwide moral and spiritual pollution of ancient society. It was a society that, humanly speaking, wearied God. His response was sweeping in its judgment: "I will blot out man whom I have created from the face of the land, from man to animals to creeping things and to birds of the sky; for I am sorry that I have made them" (v. 7).

Kill them or corrupt them! That has been the devil's strategy throughout the history of the world. Immorality, sexual perversion, pornography, child molestation—our own society bears the marks of such corruption.

The sexual relationship is a gift created by God to be enjoyed by those who are married. It represents the most satisfying kind of communication among humans and is to represent the love of Christ for His church.

Sexual relationships outside of marriage promise like a god, but in the end they pay like a devil. Satan knows this, even if our society does not. Therefore, sexual temptation is not only our most vulnerable target, but it also has the potential for the greatest heartache.

The sex goddess presents herself in movies, music, and talk shows. She promises that permissiveness is the path to happiness; she assures us that the negative consequences are well worth the lure of forbidden intimacy. She will kiss the soul, then betray the soul forever. Here are Christ's words:

> *"For the coming of the Son of Man will be just like the days of Noah. For as in those days which were before the flood they were eating and drinking, marrying and giving in marriage, until the day that Noah entered the ark, and they did not understand until the flood came and took them all away; so shall the coming of the Son of Man be."* (Matthew 24:37–39)

The success of God's promises was dependent upon the small family in the ark. If that ark had sunk to the bottom of the cold water, the promise of God would have drowned with it. Humanly speaking, Christ would not have been born in Bethlehem. He would not have died to redeem mankind, and even Adam and Eve would have suffered with Satan in hell forever.

But the ark did not sink. More accurately, it *could not* sink, for God had predicted that the seed of the woman would crush the serpent's head. The promise of God that floated along within the ark was safe. God had spoken. And if He promises, will He not do it?

The Serpent had struck with his most decisive blow, but always shy of the bull's-eye. God was one step ahead, orchestrating, planning, and outwitting. God proved that no matter how sinful the race becomes, He can always, if He wills, preserve it.

A STRIKE AGAINST THE ROYAL SEED: KILL THEM

Although Noah and his family survived the flood, their descendants soon turned away from the Lord and followed their own desires. Rather than spread out as God had commanded, many people stayed in Shinar and built a tower whose top was to "reach into heaven" (Genesis 11:4). In His displeasure, God confused their language so that they could not understand one another. The name of the place was therefore called Babel, and became the origin of occult, Babylonian worship.

Corruption was so widespread that we do not know of anyone who walked with God after the tower of Babel. Surely Satan must have rejoiced, thinking that the race was so degraded that no seed could arise to destroy him. Again, the serpent's victory appeared complete and worldwide. Imagine a world in which there is not a single righteous person!

The promise of God was enclosed there with him!

But God had other plans. He sovereignly chose a man out of idolatry to become the father of the nation from which the Redeemer would come. He proved that even those who had no righteous lineage could become followers of the Almighty when He wished to act directly in their lives. When God wanted, He could simply *choose* men to follow Him!

"Now the Lord said to Abram . . ."

With those words in Genesis 12 a whole new chapter begins in the history of redemption. Satan, who is all ears when God makes a pronouncement, gradually learned that the seed that would destroy him would come through Abraham, Isaac, Jacob, the tribe of Judah, and the family of David.

Notice how far we have come. God proved that He can, if He wishes, *multiply* the race to fulfill His promise; that He can, if He wishes, *preserve* the seed; and that He can, if He wishes, simply *choose* the seed, bringing righteousness out of unrighteousness. These and other options are always open to Him.

Before Christ was born, there was at least one other serious attempt to destroy the possibility of a coming Redeemer. Because of the promise God made to David, Satan knew that the seed of the woman would have to come through David's lineage. It was that offspring the serpent attempted to destroy.

An evil woman named Athaliah tried to exterminate the royal seed in a ruthless bid for personal power (2 Kings 11:1). Athaliah was the daughter of Ahab and Jezebel and the wife of King Jehoram of Judah who had been judged by God because of his disobedience. She perpetuated her sinister family history.

Specifically, Athaliah's sons had been killed by the pagan Philistines and Arabians (2 Chronicles 21:16–17), and now she saw the opportunity to seize the throne for herself. So she proceeded to have all of her grandsons killed, in total disregard for God's command that the descendants of David should rule over Judah forever.

But God's promise was not overturned. An aunt hid one of the seventy grandsons, so that he escaped the wrath of this evil woman. As young Joash was hiding in a closet, the promise of God was enclosed there with him! He needed to live in order that God's promise to David would come to pass. When his evil grandmother died, Joash was made king and the seed was perpetuated.

Doubtless, that nameless aunt had no idea that she was playing such a crucial role in the history of redemption. She hid the boy only because of a kind response to a tragedy. But, humanly speaking, the will and promise of God were in the balance. The integrity of God was wrapped up in the life of one frightened child, who most likely had no idea of how important he was. Once again, Satan tasted victory, but when it was in his mouth, it turned to poison.

SATAN'S WAYS; GOD'S DELAYS

Of course the battle is never as close as God allows it to appear to be. The trump cards are always held by God. Certain principles by which Satan operates are beginning to emerge.

1. *Satan's primary strategy is directed against God's people.* Those nations and religions he already has in his possession are not a threat to him. He stalks us, seeking to devour those who have believed on Christ. He knows he has to surrender the control of those whom God has chosen, and for this reason he regards God's people as his number one enemy.

In the Old Testament, his enemy was Israel, the people through whom the seed would come. In fact, in the future he will again try to exterminate the nation of Israel, so that God might not fulfill His promises that are yet unfulfilled (Revelation 12). More of that later.

In this age, the church is his enemy—and he uses the same tactics. During the first three centuries of Christianity he tried to kill the church by ten waves of persecution instigated by the polytheistic Roman Empire. But the blood of the martyrs became the seed of the church. No matter how many Christians he killed, more stood in line to take their place.

Satan's delusions feed
on the appearance of victory.

After the time of Constantine, Satan stopped trying to kill the church but instead sought to corrupt her. Now that Christianity was the official religion of the Roman Empire, everyone was Christianized and multitudes became part of the church. Many people who had followed paganism kept their practices, and a politically corrupt church embraced them. When the true followers of Christ tried to break away from the official established church, they in turn were persecuted. The heretics who were burned at the stake were often some of the most committed Christians that lived on planet Earth.

Even today, through doctrinal confusion and moral degeneration, Satan continues his relentless pursuit of the people of God. He wants us to poison our commitment to Christ through contamination from the world. He wants us to stumble so that we will lose our love for God and effectiveness in representing Christ to the world. He wants to divide us, dilute us, and destroy us.

If you are listening to the gospel, he will try to blind you; if you are already a Christian, he will seek to deceive you. His method is to convince us that God is not good, so that we will turn against Him. He comes to steal God's blessings and to make our own ways seem better than those of the Almighty. The more spiritual the man or woman, the more persistent the attacks. To destroy the faith of one believer is worth more than the tacit worship of the many unconverted who are content within the kingdom of darkness.

2. *All Satan's victories are illusory.* Pyrrhus fought a battle against Rome that inflicted so many casualties upon his army that he is said to have remarked, "If we win another battle like this one, we shall be destroyed!"

Yes, Satan does win some powerful battles. God allows him the privilege of temporarily defeating His children and sowing dissention, corruption, and, yes, even death. But bear in mind that whenever he wins, he loses, and the greater his punishment to come in the lake of fire.

Satan's delusions feed on the appearance of victory. Abel was dead, but then there was Seth. The earth was corrupted, but there was Noah. The nations turned to paganism, but then there was Abraham. Almost all of the seed was massacred, but Joash was safe in a closet. The male children of Bethlehem are massacred, but Christ escapes to Egypt. *Satan is as far from victory when he appears to have it in hand as he is when writhing in the lake of fire.*

His final humiliation and torment is as inevitable as those spirits in Tartarus who have, apparently, little to do but contemplate the fate that assuredly awaits them. They have no more victories, no more plans for fighting against God. The knowledge of their certain doom makes the Serpent of Paradise quiver. The venom with which he inflicts others returns to his own head.

3. *Our victory is real.* Our victory is genuine for one reason: We stand with Christ in His triumph. Christ invites us to participate in crushing the Serpent's head. We are the victors because Christ is.

If only we had 20/20 vision in the spirit world! When the Syrians came against Elisha intending to kill him, the prophet was giving some comfort to the terrified servant who was with him. The pagans had sent a great army of horses and chariots and surrounded Dothan, where Elisha was staying. To his attendant he gave this word of encouragement, "Do not fear, for those who are with us are more than those who are with them" (2 Kings 6:16). Then he prayed, "and the Lord opened the servant's eyes, and he saw; and behold, the mountain was full of horses and chariots of fire all around Elisha" (v. 17).

There is a story of an artist who painted a picture of a young man who was playing chess with the devil. The loser would have to become the servant of the winner. In the painting, the devil declared checkmate in three moves. The young man's pale face reflected the horror upon hearing those ominous words of certain defeat.

But a chess player, Paul Morphey, stared at the picture, studying all the configurations of the various pieces. Suddenly he shouted, "Young man, there is a move you can make!"

The painter had overlooked a possible combination of moves; it was not checkmate after all. Christ came to earth to tell us that it only *looks* as if Satan has us in his grasp.

When Satan does his worst, God does His best. In accordance with a plan worked out in the counsels of eternity, Christ came to earth to fight against the Serpent. And the Son of God declared, "Checkmate."

And Satan is fresh out of moves.

6

THE SERPENT
IS CRUSHED

There was a scuffle as the serpent thrashed about, his fangs upright, hissing at his opponent. As the loathsome beast lay gasping, it attempted to strike but could only nip the heel of the foot that stepped on its head. When the frenzy was over, the head of the serpent lay crushed, pounded into the hard dirt, its body throbbing with pain. While drops of its poison lay spent on the ground, the victor returned to heaven in triumph.

At last, Christ was here. Centuries earlier, God had said to the Serpent, "And I will put enmity between you and the woman, and between your seed and her seed; he shall bruise you on the head, and you shall bruise him on the heel" (Genesis 3:15). God had made good on His Word.

When Christ was born in Bethlehem, Satan's first strategy was to kill him. Wicked King Herod tried to carry out the diabolical deed. But Joseph and Mary took the baby to Egypt, and the plan was foiled.

If he could not kill Christ, he would seek to corrupt Him! But in the desert, Christ proved that He would not bow to satanic temptation. Try as he might, Satan could not convince Christ to take a shortcut in becoming the rightful ruler of the world. Not even Peter was able to pressure Christ into choosing life rather than death in Jerusalem. "Get thee behind me, Satan," Christ told him (Mark 8:33 KJV).

Once Satan saw that Christ was headed toward Jerusalem, he stopped trying to prevent the Cross and chose to become a key player in the drama. The reason for the switch of tactics is not difficult to understand. If Christ was going to the Cross, then the Serpent wanted the satisfaction of knowing that he had a part in it. His sadistic delight in seeing Christ hang helplessly between heaven and earth, though fleeting, was a temptation he could not resist. Yes, he knew his judgment would be greater; yes, he knew that the Cross would mean eventual defeat. But that was tomorrow. For today, he would inspire men to kill the Lord's Christ, no matter how illusory the victory.

THE CROSS, THE CONFLICT

How do we know that the Cross was a time of satanic conflict? First, Satan himself entered into Judas to betray Christ (John 13:27). Though we frequently read of demon possession in the New Testament, as the decisive conflict looms, Satan himself comes to do the dirty work. There was to be no mistake—Christ would be turned over to the political authorities of the day. Judas would be the human vehicle to do a satanic deed.

Can [God] reconcile us ... and still retain His holy integrity?

Second, Christ conceded that this was the hour for evil to take over and do its work. After Judas betrayed Him, Christ told His disciples that they should not retaliate. Then, turning to the chief priest and officers, He said, "Have you come out with swords and clubs as you would against a robber? While I was with you daily in the temple, you did not lay hands on Me; but this hour and the power of darkness are yours" (Luke 22:52–53).

"For the moment you win!"

Christ was willing to go toe-to-toe with His enemy and in effect say, "Yes, you may humiliate me. Yes, you will see me crucified naked. Yes, you will gloat over my apparent weakness." For a brief moment the Serpent would be elated. But he would celebrate too soon. If time belonged to Satan, eternity would belong to God.

Third, Christ Himself saw the Cross as the decisive victory. "Now judgment is upon this world; now the ruler of this world shall be cast out. And I, if I be lifted up from the earth, will draw all men to Myself" (John 12:31–32). Even in His "weakness," Christ would be striking the telling blow to Satan on his turf. The "ruler of this world" would be defeated in the world he claims to rule.

We've often heard that Satan was judged at the Cross. We know that he was "cast out" on this decisive battle, the focal point of history. And yet we also know that God has allowed him to continue to wield extraordinary power in this world.

What does it mean to say that the Cross crushed the head of the Serpent? And how were we included in Christ's victory?

THE CROSS, THE CONTESTANTS

The Cross, incredibly enough, is about us.

The question to be settled is whether God can reconcile us to Himself and still retain His holy integrity. To put it briefly, the issue is this: Do any of us have the right to belong to God forever despite the fact that we are members of a race that sided with Satan? Or, how can unholy people become the sons and daughters of a holy God?

There is a scene in the Old Testament that fits this dilemma exactly. Joshua, a high priest (no relation to Joshua the military commander), is pictured as standing before the Lord clothed in "filthy garments." No doubt he felt just as dirty within as he appeared to be without. Even righteous people feel sinful in the presence of God.

Then, as if Joshua's own sense of shame were not enough, we read that Satan was "standing at his right hand to accuse him." (For the whole story read Zechariah 3:1-7.) That's about all you need when you are overwhelmed with guilt and failure—the devil at your side to whisper in your ear how bad you really are! He who is more wicked than we could ever be is on hand to judge our wickedness!

But this story does paint an accurate picture of our predicament. The fact is, we also are "filthy"—a strong word, but one that is apt when we stand in God's presence. And Satan does accuse us, insisting that we have no right to belong to God. We can be thankful that God has a remedy for the moral distance that exists between us and Him. He says to us, just as he did to sinful Joshua, "See, I have taken your iniquity away from you and will clothe you with festal robes" (Zechariah 3:4).

Imagine a courtroom scene. God is judge, Satan is the accuser, and we stand in Joshua's shoes. The question arises: What can be done to help us pitiful sinners as we stand in God's presence? If something is to be done, God must do it. Unless he acquits us, and figuratively speaking gives us those clothes of righteousness, we would be cast aside. After all, Satan does have a point. We are sinners who don't deserve to be loved and accepted by God.

Take note that the conflict between God and Satan is always waged over us; we are the trophies. If we are believers in Christ, Satan knows he cannot have our souls, but he will try to destroy our fellowship with God. Satan will do all that He can to dispute God's plans and judgment. But God will always win the battle for those who are His.

Just how He won that battle for us is the subject of this chapter. Giving us "festal robes" so that we no longer need be under the Serpent's domain involved an ingenious plan. And Satan, our accuser, who talks when he should be silent, was struck dumb.

THE CROSS, THE COURTROOM

How I wish a video camera had been able to record the drama that took place in the spiritual world when Christ died on the cross! A cosmic battle was being fought. The devil was there, God was there, and Christ was there—and so were we. Just read Paul's words, keeping in mind that we will explain the details in a moment.

When you were dead in your transgressions and the uncircumcision of your flesh, He made you alive together with Him, having forgiven us all our transgressions, having canceled out the certificate of debt consisting of decrees against us, which was hostile to us; and He has taken it out of the way, having nailed it to the cross. When He had disarmed the rulers and authorities, He made a public display of them, having triumphed over them through Him. (Colossians 2:13–15)

To unravel this passage, we must turn again to a courtroom scene, describing the key players, pinpointing the issues, and reporting the outcome. All the while, we must remember that it is our eternity that hangs in the balance. Don't forget, this is about us.

The Accusation

For openers, we are sinners, both by nature and by choice. We have all felt the agitation of a troubled conscience. But the sins we can remember are only a small part of the sum total of our guilt before God. Paul wants us to feel the full weight of the charges against us, or at least to be reminded of how far-reaching they really are.

He describes God's law, which we have broken, as "the certificate of debt consisting of decrees against us, which was hostile to us" (Colossians 2:14). Whether we know it or not, God's commandments have a claim over us. We are not free to write our own rules for the simple reason that God has already written them. But these laws were "hostile" to us; before them we stand condemned. So these decrees had to be taken out of the way before fellowship with God was possible.

In the courts of Paul's day, if you were brought before a judge, there had to be a hearing where the accused would be interrogated to see whether there was enough evidence to warrant a trial (today, we are more sophisticated and call it a grand jury). Recall that when accusations were made against Christ, Pilate questioned Him to see whether he deserved a hearing. When he saw that the charges were false, he said to the multitude, "I have found no guilt in this man" (Luke 23:14). Nevertheless, Pilate's cowardice led him to submit to the cries of the mob.

In our case, God does not have to ask us questions to probe for clues of guilt or innocence. He knows much better than we the extent of our guilt. That is why Paul says that in the presence of God's law "every mouth [is] closed, and all the world [is] accountable to God" (Romans 3:19). So we stand in shameful silence. No words escape our lips.

The devil, our accuser, is not quite as controlled. He speaks and has much to say. I believe he still has access to heaven today and is angry when we stand whole and clean on this earth, enjoying the presence of God. He reminds God of His promise that "the soul who sins will die" (Ezekiel 18:4). As an accuser, he quite possibly approaches God with a list of our sins; he comes armed with reasons we should be cast away from the divine presence. Let us never forget that his accusation is just. God Himself has said that "the wages of sin is death" (Romans 6:23). This time, Satan speaks at least some truth.

Of course Satan does not tell God anything that the Almighty does not already know. In fact, God knows more about us than Satan could ever comprehend. The dispute is not whether we have committed sins or not. The matter at hand is not whether we are as bad as Satan says we are. Rather, the controversy is over what should be done about our predicament.

Satan says, "You should *damn* him!"

God says, "I will *save* him!"

Perhaps we should pause to remind ourselves that the charges against us are not only accurate but extensive. In God's court we do not have to steal to be considered a thief, do not have to commit adultery to be considered an adulterer, and do not have to fashion a god to be an idolater. All that we need to do is to fantasize, desiring to do these things. What is more, we not only sin, but we are actually sinners; that is, we are seen as being in a state of sin. Nothing is hidden.

Not surprisingly, Satan insists that if we are allowed into heaven, we will defile its courts. God, he says, could be accused of associating with men who are unclean. Indeed, both the reputation and the truthfulness of God would be questioned. After all, it was the Almighty Himself who proclaimed His holiness and warned that sin brings death.

Satan's accusation against us follows one of two directions. Objectively he accuses us before God, arguing that we are too sinful to be acquitted. Subjectively he preys on our consciences, trying to make us feel so guilty that we shy away from God's grace. He who lures us into sin turns to condemn us for doing his bidding. And if that doesn't work, he will reverse himself and make us feel so good about ourselves that we believe we do not need God's grace at all.

Satan's one objective is to keep us separated from fellowship with God. He wants us to be on our own, just as he is. On our own, with him at our side!

The Penalty

Satan insists, perhaps quite reasonably, that we should have the same judgment as he. After all, we also are tainted with sin and are also rebels. If the greatness of the sin is determined by the greatness of the One against whom it is committed, then, indeed, we are supremely guilty. Let us be judged along with the Serpent, since we have a drop of the Serpent's poison.

Satan knew that he could count on God to hold fast to His standard of righteousness. He who had served as the Almighty's primary representative was confident that if His Master did not waver in His high standards, mankind would be abandoned to hell. Yes, the Evil One knew that God was loving, but He also knew that His love could neither override nor cancel His justice. There could be no exceptions, even for people who did the best they could in this life.

Satan thought it was unfair that men could be eternally saved while he was eternally damned. Satan's point, which seems reasonable enough, is that each being should pay for his own sin; that would be just. After all, that is what Satan had to do. Sin is sin. Justice is justice. And God is God.

The ingenious plan Satan could not foresee is that, in the case of humans, one human would die for other humans. Specifically, one infinite human would die for a group of finite ones. God would thus keep His promise that "the soul who sins will die" (Ezekiel 18:4)—but someone else would do the dying. The wages of sin would still be death, but someone else would die in our stead.

Liberal theologians have often criticized the biblical teaching that Christ died for sinners by saying that it would be immoral for God to punish an innocent person on behalf of a guilty one. The answer, however, is that Christ was not innocent. He was made sin for us: "He made Him who knew no sin to be sin on our behalf, that we might be made the righteousness of God in Him"

(2 Corinthians 5:21). Christ was declared to be a sinner, although He had never sinned; and we were declared to be saints, although we are decidedly "unsaintly."

Yes, Christ was regarded as a sinner; He became legally guilty of all of our sins, from lying to genocide. He was deemed guilty of unimaginable crimes. Because His guilt and punishment was *real*, we have a *real* Savior who can save us from some very *real* sins.

When was Christ "made sin for us"? Not in the Garden of Gethsemane, although Christ suffered there in deep agony and sorrow. Not when the crown of thorns was placed on His brow and the blood flowed from His forehead to his chin and then dripped onto His chest. Only when Christ was on the cross did the transaction take place. When He shed His blood and actually died, we were redeemed.

Let us not overlook this comment in the book of Deuteronomy: "And if a man has committed a sin worthy of death, and he is put to death, and you hang him on a tree, his corpse shall not hang all night on the tree, but you shall surely bury him on the same day (for he who is hanged is accursed of God), so that you do not defile your land which the Lord your God gives you as an inheritance" (Deuteronomy 21:22–23). Christ had to be hung, crucified on the cross, before He could be declared cursed of God in our behalf. The moment He was placed there, He drew upon Himself the wrath of God. Paul put it clearly. "Christ redeemed us from the curse of the Law, having become a curse for us—for it is written, 'Cursed is everyone who hangs on a tree'" (Galatians 3:13).

Only when the nails were put through His hands, only when the cross was lifted up with His body hanging on it, only when He breathed His last could God's wrath, which was stored up against sin, be expended. God the Father could not look upon one who was so thoroughly accursed. This separation, this anger directed toward His beloved Son, caused the anguished cry, "My God, my God, why hast thou forsaken me?" (Matthew 27:46 KJV). Thus we have a Savior.

Let's look at this transaction through Paul's imagery. He says the decrees that were against us were "nailed. . . . to the cross" (Colossians 2:14). In those days, when a criminal was hung on the cross, his crime had to be publicly proclaimed. The list of transgressions was written on a placard and nailed above the dying man. Recall that Pilate put a notice above Christ's head with the accusation, "JESUS THE NAZARENE, THE KING OF THE JEWS" (John 19:19). He wrote it in three languages—Hebrew, Greek, and Latin (v. 20). He wanted everyone to see the crime Christ was accused of committing.

It is true, of course, that Christ was the king of the Jews; in this, Pilate's words and God's verdict agreed. Needless to say, however, this hardly deserved punishment. It was not a crime to speak the truth. Yes, Christ was the king of the Jews, but it was not for this that He was dying.

High above Pilate's words, there was a cosmic bulletin board on which our sins were listed. Though I wasn't born yet, the sins that I would commit two thousand years later were recorded there. The list included everything that Satan had said about us as well as other secret sins that were known but to God. Only the Almighty knows how long the list of accusations was; only He knows the extent of our sin and the severity of its penalty.

God, then, did not see Christ as dying for His own crimes; nor, for that matter, was Christ a victim of circumstances that got out of control. He was delivered by the "predetermined plan and foreknowledge of God" to redeem sinners (Acts 2:23). "But He was pierced through for our transgressions, He was crushed for our iniquities; the chastening for our well-being fell upon Him, and by His scourging we are healed. . . . But the Lord was pleased to crush Him, putting Him to grief" (Isaiah 53:5, 10).

The penalty was just. And the penalty was fully paid.

The Verdict

God has pronounced us *forgiven!*

With the accusations against us taken out of the way, God maintained His holiness and yet acquitted us. As Paul says, He has "forgiven us all our transgressions" (Colossians 2:13).

God made no secret of Christ's success. Ancient Rome had a victory parade when the soldiers returned from a successful battle. The victors not only marched with the captive prisoners of war in tow, but they displayed the goods captured in battle. The Romans gloated in victory, choosing the main highway to enter the city. Just so, Satan's defeat was a public event, not to us, but to the entire spirit world. To quote Paul again, "When He had disarmed the rulers and authorities, He made a public display of them [the rulers and authorities]" (Colossians 2:15).

Satan was thus publicly disarmed. In Greek, the word translated *disarmed* means "stripped of weapons." Christ stripped him of his presumptuous insistence that he could continue to fight against Him and be successful. Satan was shorn of his pride and his supposed right to hold us as subjects in his kingdom. Though our mouths were closed in the presence of Satan's accusations, his mouth is now closed in the presence of our acquittal.

The victory of Christ does not mean, however, that Satan can no longer fight against us. Think of it this way. God stripped King Saul of his title as king even though he was still allowed to harass King David for ten long years. Although the forces who war against us had their authority removed, they continue to fight. They prefer to live in denial rather than face the humiliation of defeat.

In *Satan Cast Out,* Frederick S. Leahy says that it is only from our standpoint that there seems to be a gap between the victory of Christ over Satan and the final disposal of the defeated foe. He reminds us that lightning and thunder take place at the same time, but we see the light before we hear the rumble. He writes:

> In objective reality, these are virtually one, but from our standpoint, owing to the fact that light travels more quickly than sound, there is usually a time-lag between seeing the flash and hearing the thunder. With God, the victory and the judgment are all in the cross.[1]

We can say that we have seen the lightning, but we have not yet heard the crash of his fall. With God, there is no such gap; He regards the judgment and sentence as already complete. *"Now* the ruler of this world will be cast out" (John 12:31; italics added). And again, "The ruler of this world *has been judged"* (John 16:11, italics added).

THE SPECIFICS OF CHRIST'S VICTORY

How, then, did Christ defeat Satan at the Cross?

Christ Reconciled Sinners to God—Permanently

Christ satisfied our debt so completely and justly that we who believe in Christ no longer owe God any righteousness. Since the penalty for sin was not life but death, Christ had to die and in so doing reconciled us to God forever.

Consider that phrase once more: "having forgiven . . . all our transgressions" (Colossians 2:13). How many of your sins were future when Christ died two thousand years ago? Obviously, all of them, since not a one of us had yet been born. God anticipated our sin and included it in Christ's death. Christ not only died for the sins of the Old Testament saints but also for those who would become saints in the future. As the song goes, "I was on His mind when He died."

Now let me take the logic a step further. What about the sins you will still commit tomorrow and the day after? The answer, of course, is that for those who believe on Christ, even those sins have already been forgiven. It must be so, for if when we received Christ we were only forgiven for our past sins, we could not be sure of our future salvation. The reason we know we will go to heaven when we die is that God has forgiven our sins—past, present, and future.

Of course, we must still confess our sins, not to maintain our status as sons but to maintain fellowship with our Father. Legally, all of our sins have been taken away. We can rejoice in the security of our salvation because we have been acquitted, completely and forever.

The author of Hebrews put it this way: "But He, having offered one sacrifice for sins for all time, sat down at the right hand of God. . . . For by one offering He has perfected for all time those who are sanctified" (Hebrews 10:12, 14).

One High Priest, *one* offering, *one* act of justification whereby we are declared righteous. As He did with Joshua, God gives us clothes to wear that cover our sins:

> Jesus, Thy blood and righteousness
> My beauty art; my glorious dress;
> 'Midst flaming worlds in these arrayed,
> With joy shall I lift up my head.

For those who do not accept Christ as their substitute, Satan's original indictment stands. But for those who believe, we have been taken out from Satan's kingdom and have been transferred into the kingdom of Christ.

Christ Silenced Satan

Satan's mouth was shut. His whimpering accusations stopped. The Judge of all the earth had declared us righteous—who was Satan to say otherwise? Can the failed god contradict the Lord of heaven and earth? To free men, Christ had to win a victory over the accuser of men. He who tried to keep men and women in bondage had to be exposed, his power destroyed, and his prisoners set free.

In biblical times, if a placard of the man's crimes were put on his prison cell, it was returned to him when he had served his punishment. When he was allowed to take it home, it was no longer an indictment but a trophy! Across it was written *Tetelesti*, that is, "Paid in full."

If a neighbor asked him whether he was legally free, he could show him the document. The debt of justice had been served. There was nothing left to pay. Significantly, Christ's last words from the cross were *tetelesti*, translated "It is finished" (John 19: 30). Our debt was "paid in full."

> Jesus paid it all,
> All to Him I owe;
> Sin had left a crimson stain,
> He washed it white as snow.

If God were still to expect a payment from us after Christ paid our debt, there would be unrighteousness with God. Our debt was paid so fully that no further payment will ever be necessary. This is why we can say, "There is therefore now no condemnation to them which are in Christ Jesus."

Recently a woman wrote to tell me about her bad marriage. She ended by saying, "I've given up trying to please God. If I can't please my father and my husband, I will never please Him."

How would you have answered? I wrote back, "I have some good news for you: You do not have to try to please God; God is already more pleased with Christ than He could ever be with you or me, even if we have several good days in a row! If you trust

Christ, God is as pleased with you as He is with His blessed Son whom He dearly loves."

Of course this must be balanced with the equally true challenge of Scripture that we should strive to please God (1 Corinthians 9:24–27; 2 Timothy 2:4). But we cannot please Him until we know that He is already pleased with us. Only when we know that we are His beloved children in "whom He is well-pleased" are we at peace, able to live desiring to please God in our daily experience.

On particularly difficult days I have prayed, "O, God, today please do not look on me at all, look only upon your Son and see me as complete in Him." I know that God also wants me to become like His Son in everyday living, but I will never please God as Christ has; therefore, I delight to rest in His work on my behalf.

I often receive letters from people who believe that they have committed the "unpardonable sin." Now of course, there is an "unpardonable sin"; it is the sin of unbelief, the hardness of heart that often accompanies those who have heard the gospel message but are determined to reject it.

But no Christian can commit the "unpardonable sin." Those who have transferred their trust to Christ have had their sins pardoned. Christ has canceled all of our transgressions. He knew us long before we were born; He knew the evil we would do; and He covered it all.

When Satan accuses us, we must show him our canceled certificate and read aloud, "Paid in full." We must say to him, "Begone! for it is written, 'Who will bring a charge against God's elect? God is the one who justifies; who is the one who condemns? Christ Jesus is He who died, yes, rather who was raised, who is at the right of God, who also intercedes for us'" (Romans 8:33–34).

Our attorney, Christ, has pleaded our case, and God has accepted His plea. And when God speaks, the universe listens.

Christ Proved He Had the Power of Life

Satan can only kill; he cannot make alive.

In order for God to prove His complete superiority, He had to raise Christ up from the dead so that there would never be any dispute over who was Lord and King. For this reason, the resurrection of Christ is a necessary part of the gospel message (1 Corinthians 15:3–5). Death, which is itself the consequence of sin, was fearful, but Christ conquered it for us. "Since then the children share in flesh and blood, He Himself likewise also partook of the same, that through death He might render powerless him who had the power of death, that is, the devil; and might deliver those who through fear of death were subject to slavery all their lives" (Hebrews 2:14).

Of course Satan never had the power to determine when a person would die. Such matters belong to the risen Christ, who won the honor of possessing the keys of death and Hades. Satan does, however, hold the tyranny of death over our heads; and in the case of the unconverted, death slams the door of opportunity to believe in Christ.

A butterfly was observed inside a windowpane, fluttering in great fright. It was pursued by a sparrow who kept pecking at the butterfly, eager to devour it. What the butterfly could not see was the pane of glass that separated the two of them. The butterfly did not realized that he was as safe next to the sparrow as he would have been he had flown to the South Pole. Just so, the invisible Christ comes to shield us from Satan's power. The Serpent can hiss and taunt, but he cannot devour. We have a different King; we serve in a different kingdom.

Christ came to deliver us from the fear of life and the fear of death. His resurrection proved that He was stronger than the grave. And when He ascended into heaven, He opened its gates for all who would believe on Him.

Christ Opened the Gates of Heaven

Not all Bible scholars agree, but I believe that those who died in faith in the Old Testament went to hades, and not until the Ascension of Christ were they taken up to heaven. Paul wrote that when Christ ascended, "He led captive a host of captives, and He gave gifts to men" (Ephesians 4:8). Perhaps that means that those who were in the righteous compartment of hades were taken to heaven at that time.

Regardless, of this we can be sure: Christ's death opened heaven to those who are His children. To the thief on the cross He could say, "Today you shall be with Me in Paradise" (Luke

23:43). There is now a direct route to heaven, opened by One who Himself has entered. Death no longer is our enemy but a friend that takes us to God.

When a little girl was asked why she was not afraid to walk through the cemetery, she answered, "Because my home is on the other side." Once a bee has stung its victim, it cannot strike a second time. It can only annoy and terrify, but its sting has been exhausted. Christ took the sting out of death and assures us that "to be absent from the body [is to be] present with the Lord" (2 Corinthians 5:8 KJV).

When Stephen was stoned, he could already see Christ waiting for his arrival. Indeed, the Son of God stood to welcome His faithful child home. The gates of heaven await all who believe.

Christ Exalted Us Above the Angelic Realm

Would you change places with the angel Gabriel? Think before you answer. We might be tempted to envy a being that had such beauty and power. We just might think that he is a cut above us. True, we can never approach the strength and beauty of an angel. We cannot even imagine what it would be like to fly through the universe doing assignments for God.

> **We will have an honor beyond what he enjoyed.**

And yet, we shall be above the angels. No angel can ever be called a brother of Christ. It follows that no angel can ever be an "heir of Christ." For a little time Christ became lower than the angels, for no angel has ever died. For a little time we are lower than the angels, but that too will change (Hebrews 2:5–13).

Again we must return to God's eternal perspective. God has taken us from the pit to walk in the palace "that the manifold wisdom of God might now [since the Cross] be made known through the church to the rulers and authorities in the heavenly places" (Ephesians 3:10). Put simply, God wanted to show off His grace. So He took sinners who had fallen so low and exalted them so high!

> We are to judge the world;
> We are to judge angels;
> We are to be heirs of God and joint heirs of Christ.

No wonder Satan is furious. The fact that we will have an honor beyond what he enjoyed before his fall from grace is more than his envious nature can tolerate. Think of all that he had already given up. He could no longer be a prophet who could speak for God. He could no longer be a priest who would direct worship to God. He could no longer be a messenger bearing messages for God. He who wished to be like God has ended up the most unlike Him. In short, it was all loss and no gain.

Today he is out on bail. He is allowed to roam until his final judgment. The sentence to the lake of fire has only been postponed. The verdict has already been read. We have seen the lightning. The thunder is on its way.

My wife and I have visited the Wartburg Castle in Germany, where Martin Luther spent ten months in hiding. There, in a small room, perhaps no bigger than fifteen feet square, he anguished, often feeling the attacks of Satan. Tradition says that in that room he threw his inkwell at the devil. Perhaps his comment in the *Table Talks* gives a different interpretation of the event, when he said, "I fought the devil with ink." He may have meant that he fought the devil by translating the New Testament into German.

We can be quite sure that his attacks from Satan were many. Yet the strength and safety of the Wartburg and other fortresses gave him the inspiration to write his famous hymn, "A Mighty Fortress Is Our God." One of the stanzas reads:

> And though this world, with devils filled,
> Should threaten to undo us,
> We will not fear, for God hath willed
> His truth to triumph through us.
> The prince of darkness grim—

We tremble not for him;
His rage we can endure,
For lo! his doom is sure,
One little word shall fell him.

And what is that "little word"? It is the six-letter word *Christ*. Christ, properly understood, can "fell him."

The Cross proved it.

If we ask why Satan has not already been consigned to the pit, the answer is that God is using him to complete the divine plan. As we shall see in the next chapter, the Serpent is actually God's servant. He served before he fell and he is serving even now. He has a different motivation, and the conditions are far worse than they once were, but he is a servant nonetheless.

And with that we lift the curtain on the next chapter in our drama.

7

THE SERPENT, GOD'S SERVANT

How much power do you think Satan has?

We might think that we can't give a precise answer to that question because we don't know exactly what our enemy can and cannot do. After all, we are talking about a being we have never seen and whose powers are in realms beyond us. And yet, looked at another way, the question can be answered accurately: The devil has exactly as much power as God lets him have, and not one mite more!

Sometimes I think the devil enjoys much of the renewed attention he has received in the last twenty years! Go into any bookstore, whether Christian or secular, and you will find shelves of books about him. Mind you, I think that biblical teaching about the devil is necessary; after all, the Scriptures have much to say about him. My point is simply that in much of the literature his ability to wield power is grossly overestimated.

Of course, many of us can remember when the church fell into the opposite error. Satan was not taken seriously. He was known to be our foe, but most Christians believed they had never been directly affected by him. You could scarcely find a counselor who would conclude that a personal problem was actually rooted in a "demonic stronghold." Even clear instances of demon possession were diagnosed under a different label.

Some teachers, having finally understood that we all are affected by Satan or one of his emissaries, have made demonic exorcism to be the primary means of breaking stubborn habits or dealing with a painful past. At best, Satan is found to be the cause of virtually every problem; at worst, he has been thought to be well-nigh all-powerful. Rather than inspiring faith, such counseling has led to helpless pessimism. Oh, yes, God will win in the end, but in this world, we are told, Satan has free reign to do whatever he wishes. Though most agree that at the end of the day God will win, some people live and talk as if it will be a close finish. Well, it won't be!

I shall say it one more time: The devil is just as much God's servant in his rebellion as he was God's servant in the days of his sweet obedience. Even today, he cannot act without God's express permission; he can neither tempt, coerce, demonize, nor make so much as a single plan without the consent and approval of God. We can't quote Luther too often: The devil is God's devil!

He is not the devil you might have heard about.

Satan has different roles to play, depending on God's counsel and purposes. He is pressed into service to do God's will in the world; he must do the bidding of the Almighty. We must bear in mind that he does have frightful powers, but knowing that those can only be exercised under God's direction and pleasure gives us hope. Satan is simply not free to wreak havoc on people at will.

Yes, if God had so chosen, He could have banished the fallen servant to another planet or sent him directly to the lake of fire. Either of those plans or any other that God would choose would be right and just. But God kept Satan in this world for one reason: Satan had to play his part in the drama on planet Earth, and he will play it according to God's rules and not his own.

Why is it important that we know this? That God might be

rightly honored as King of kings, as God, the ruler of heaven and earth. God created Lucifer before he became the devil. It was God who cursed the Serpent. It was God who predicted his ultimate defeat and humiliation. It was God who allowed the devil to fight against Christ. And it will be God who will supervise the conflict to the very end. God has not abandoned His responsibility of being in charge of all of His creation, even that part that has foolishly chosen to stand against Him.

We must also be reminded of Satan's limitations that we might fight against him in faith. The more secure we are in the knowledge that the devil is not autonomous (that is, capable of acting independently), the more faith will arise in our hearts so that we can defeat him. He is not the devil you might have heard about in the latest TV talk show or read about in the latest book.

Here are some ways in which the Serpent serves God.

GOD USES SATAN TO JUDGE THE UNCONVERTED

Now that we know that Satan is limited by God's power, we might think that God would confine his role to relatively few battles on earth: an occasional burst of flurry here, an attack there. Many people are startled to discover that Satan is allowed to cause spiritual blindness throughout the world in the minds of those who will not embrace the good news of the gospel. Interestingly, Paul wrote that our gospel is veiled to those who are perishing, "in whose case the god of this world has blinded the minds of the unbelieving, that they might not see the light of the gospel of the glory of Christ, who is the image of God" (2 Corinthians 4:4).

If that doesn't convince you that Satan is allowed to stifle the ability of the unsaved to hear the gospel, then consider the words of Christ. He said the Word of God is like a seed planted on different kinds of soils. One of these soils is so hard that the seed cannot penetrate at all. Here is Christ's explanation: "These are the ones who are beside the road where the word is sown; and when they hear, immediately Satan comes and takes away the word which has been sown in them" (Mark 4:15). He can take some thoughts out of their minds!

What is God's purpose in this work of the enemy? It is to affirm that all of us serve a god of some kind. If we are not united with the true God through Christ, we will be blinded by the false god,

Satan. We must walk in the light or be overcome by the darkness. Those who harden their hearts find them to be doubly hardened.

This blindness, however, is subject to the will and purposes of God. In the case of those who believe, God overcomes their blindness with the light of the gospel, and there is nothing the devil can do about it. A thousand devils cannot keep a soul from believing in Christ if God has chosen to grant such a one the gift of life. This power was the imagery that fired the imagination of Charles Wesley when he wrote.

> Long my imprisoned spirit lay
> Fast bound in sin and nature's night;
> Thine eye diffused a quick'ning ray,
> I woke, the dungeon flamed with light;
> My chains fell off, my heart was free;
> I rose, went forth, and followed Thee.

What is our role in helping people "see the light"? The answer is to share the Good News of the gospel with them. Paul says that this message is "the power of God for salvation to everyone who believes" (Romans 1:16). We must rely on the Holy Spirit to do what we cannot; Christ assured us that those who were given to Him by the Father would indeed come to Him and be received (John 6:35).

That Satan is given a measure of power in the minds of the unconverted should not discourage us from explaining the gospel to them. No matter how blind or spiritually dead a given individual might be, our confidence is in God's ability to open his or her heart. Whether the gospel is accepted or not, it will always be used by God in some way.

Using the imagery of the ancient Roman triumphal entries, Paul wrote that we march as it were in triumph, and the smell of our victory delights the hearts of those who belong to God, but is a curse to those who are lost. "We are a fragrance of Christ to God among those who are being saved and among those who are perishing; to the one an aroma of death unto death, to another an aroma of life unto life. And who is adequate for these things?" (2 Corinthians 2:15–16).

On the surface we might think that Satan's measure of control in the lives of the unconverted serves his own purposes. After all, what could delight him more than blinding people to God's light? But we have already learned that when he serves his own purposes, the Serpent is in reality serving God's purposes. God has His plan that is being worked out, part of which includes the judgment and fate of the unconverted. Let us affirm with confidence that Satan cannot dictate to God, but God always dictates to him.

To be God's instrument of judgment in the lives of the unconverted is to serve God. And when we remember that Satan himself will be judged for what he does, though he does it with God's permission, we are reminded even here that Satan loses even when he appears to win.

GOD USES SATAN TO REFINE THE OBEDIENT

Sometimes God chooses the scene of our battles with Satan. Does Satan wish to tempt Job to discredit the faith of this man of God? He must come to God to receive permission. In fact, it is God who brings up the subject of Job's piety as He and Satan were having what just might be a regular briefing. "Have you considered My servant Job?" God asks. "For there is no one like him on the earth, a blameless and upright man, fearing God and turning away from evil" (Job 1:8).

After an extended discussion regarding Job's possible motives for obedience, God gives Satan permission to afflict Job, but only within specific parameters. "Behold, all that he has is in your power, only do not put forth your hand on him" (v. 12). We stand in amazement at the power of Satan. He causes lightning to kill Job's servants; evil armies are raised up to destroy other servants and the animals; and last but not least, Satan causes a wind that demolishes the house in which Job's children are eating, and all ten of them are killed!

Job, as you know, maintains his integrity. "Then Job arose and tore his robe and shaved his head, and he fell to the ground and worshiped. . . . 'The Lord gave and the Lord has taken away. Blessed be the name of the Lord'" (vv. 20–21). Job passes the test, but there is more to come. Now Satan complains to God that Job was able to maintain his faith because he was not personally touched. "Skin for skin! Yes, all that a man has he will give for his life. However, put forth Your hand now, and touch his bone and his flesh; he will curse You to Your face" (2:4–5).

Mark this well: Satan's power over Job is now increased, but only because God willed it so. The Almighty gives Satan permission to smite Job with sore boils from the soles of his feet to the crown of his head. We should never underestimate Satan's power; we can, however, be sure that his power, no matter how fearsome, can only be exercised under the hand of God.

Did Job's trial come from God or the devil? The answer, of course, is that the *immediate* cause was Satan, but the *ultimate* cause was God. That is why Job's family "comforted him for all the adversities that the *Lord* had brought on him" (42:11; italics added). Since Satan can only touch God's children with the Almighty's approval, Job's trial was ultimately from the hand of his Father in heaven.

If we are in awe of Satan's power to maim, destroy, and even kill, we must never forget that he did not choose to do this on his own; or better, if he chose to do it, he had to receive God's permission before he could carry it out. The devil might be "the god of this world," but he can rule only by the divine will. Luther was right when he said that the devil's power is "as big as the world, as wide as the world, and he extends from heaven down into hell"; then he adds, "But the evil spirit has not a hairbreadth more power over us than God's goodness permits."

Sometimes Satan chooses the scene of our battles with him. When Satan observed a weakness in Peter that he wanted to exploit, he had to come to Christ and beg permission. "Simon, Simon, behold, Satan has demanded permission to sift you like wheat; but I have prayed for you, that your faith may not fail; and you, when once you have turned again, strengthen your brothers" (Luke 22:31–32). Satan had a sinister plan for Peter, but he had to check with Christ first. He could not approach Peter without divine approval. Indeed, the idea in the passage is "Satan has obtained you by asking." There he is imploring Christ for an opportunity to touch one of the Master's disciples. Satan blew all of his winds at Peter; the chaff was taken out, and only the wheat remained.

Recently I was counseling a Christian couple who feared that a curse might have been put upon them by an evil acquaintance who sought their destruction. I pointed out that if it were so, Satan would have to come to God and ask permission to touch them. Curse or no curse, the lives of Christians are not in the hands of Satan but in the hands of the Lord. Satan is paralyzed, unable to touch us, unless God gives the command.

Satan, I am convinced, wants us to think of him differently. He wants us to believe that he has independent power. If that is our understanding, we are caught off guard, filled with fear that the enemy of our souls might be acting when God isn't even watching. Or at least, we might think, God has given Satan independent powers that are unreported and unsupervised.

A woman in our congregation, the victim of occult/sexual abuse, is now a Christian, saved out of a life of horrid memories of childhood terror. She feared a curse that had been placed upon her, an oath that she was to die at the age of forty-six, the age at which her satanic father died. When it dawned on her that Satan could not act independently of God, when she understood that he could not afflict her unless God willed it, her fearful heart was at rest. Even if God does give Satan permission to strike her down at the age of forty-six, she will die not according to Satan's will but according to God's will. But as I write, she has reached the age of forty-six and is confident that her life will extend well beyond the supposed deadline.

Who do we think Satan is, if we think that he, not God, determines the day of our death? Let it be clearly affirmed: Our lives are not in Satan's hands, but in God's hands. Satan cannot act apart from divine providence. Death need not terrify us. Christ, not the devil, said, "Do not be afraid; I am the first and the last, and the living One; and I was dead, and behold, I am alive forevermore, and I have the keys of death and of Hades" (Revelation 1:17–18).

I have met Christians who have been paralyzed in their Christian life because there was occultism (and therefore idolatry) in their family line. Some think they must live the rest of their lives under a cloud, that a curse will follow them until they die. One Christian man told me that his children and grandchildren would have to live without the full blessing of God because there were no Christians in his family going back to the third and fourth generation. His text, as you might guess, was taken from the longer version of the ten commandments:

You shall not worship them or serve them; for I, the Lord your God, am a jealous God, visiting the iniquity of the fathers on the children, on the third and the fourth generations of those who hate Me, but showing lovingkindness to thousands, to those who love Me and keep My commandments. (Exodus 20:5–6)

To what extent are the iniquities of the father "visited upon the children"? There might well be generational spirits who concentrate on various family lines, exploiting the weaknesses of the offspring of idolatrous parents. But the balancing fact is that there are all kinds of spiritually minded Christians who grew up in abusive, hateful, and idolatrous families. Such a curse can only have control over us if we think we must be subject to it.

My observation has been that it is very difficult to establish a clear pattern of demonic struggles based on family history. In the passage in Exodus, the curse is only upon those who hate God. Indeed, it might be referring only to those children who hate God. In addition, God does show blessings to the thousands of those who fear Him.

No matter your family history, believers are not under a curse, for Christ bore our curse. The transformation from the kingdom of darkness into the kingdom of light was complete. Satan wants us to be preoccupied with his control, curses, and "unavoidable schemes." But like Pilate of old, he has no power against us except that which is given him from above.

A friend of mine tells the story of how his son had an unseen friend who told him, "God hates you, but if you follow me I will do you good." The boy called on this "friend" in times of trouble, not even realizing that it was an evil spirit. When the parents learned more about this strange friendship, they rebuked the demon in the name of Christ. Of course there was a battle, but the demon was routed, for one good reason: The parents knew what some do not, namely, that demons have no such rights to haunt a child.

What was God's purpose in giving a demon the power to trouble this child? Think of what the parents learned about the power of God, and what the child learned about the deceptive nature of evil and the love of Christ. Like Peter, who fell for Satan's wiles but then "strengthened his brethren," so this family is the better for the experience. Satan chose a battlefield and lost.

Today you can break a curse by affirming that Christ alone owns your life. Do not believe the lie that Satan has a right to you if you have been purchased at high cost by the blood of Christ. Accept the battles you have had as from God for your refinement and eventual blessing. We have been "rescued . . . from the domain of darkness, and transferred to the kingdom of His beloved Son" (Colossians 1:13). Rejecting the devil's lies by affirming who we are in Christ is part of our spiritual development.

Martin Luther had a servant who lived in despair because she had "sold her soul to the devil." Luther answered her by asking, "What if you were to write a bill of sale, agreeing to sell one of my children as a slave. Would that agreement have any value?"

"No, of course not, I have no right to sell a child who does not belong to me!"

To which Luther, in effect, replied, "And you are now one of God's children, since He owns your soul it cannot be given away to another." His point, of course, was that we cannot sell someone else's child. Those who belong to Christ's kingdom can never be bound by an agreement to a king who has no rights to them. Thus, by definition, all agreements and oaths made by a child of God to the devil are null and void the moment they are made.

Satan does not want you to know that, of course. He will do all that he can to make his grip formidable. But you must remember that you do not face your struggles alone. You face them with the people of God. You face them with the promises of God. "What shall we say to these things? If God is for us, who is against us?" (Romans 8:31). Remember, Satan will take all the power our unbelief gives to him.

As parents we have all taken our children to the zoo. As we have walked past the lion's cage, the children are frightened, but we aren't. That is because children usually look at the lion, but the parents usually look at the bars.

Satan is a roaring lion, seeking whom he may devour (1 Peter 5:8). Apparently he roars to frighten us; he stalks and plots against us. But like the lion at the zoo, he is only free within the parameters of his cage. He roams only where God permits. That does not mean that he has already been bound in the abyss. As we will learn later, this is a future event in which his activity on earth is curtailed completely. I simply mean that even now, God draws the lines and says, "This far and no farther." He must stay behind the bars God has ordained.

GOD USES SATAN TO DISCIPLINE THE DISOBEDIENT

Sometimes we choose the scene of the battle. Scholars debate whether King Saul should be classified as an Old Testament believer or an unbeliever. There is evidence on both sides of the ledger. Only God knows for sure.

As for me, I think there is evidence that he was indeed a believer. I suspect that Saul will be with us someday in heaven. Despite his marred track record, we read that the Spirit of the Lord came upon him mightily and he was changed into another man (1 Samuel 10:6). He had his moments of greatness, humility, and restraint.

But when David enters his life, jealousy eats him alive. What really galled Saul was the Goliath incident. Not only did David have the courage to do what Saul was too fearful to attempt, but the people fell hopelessly in love with the young man who used his sling so skillfully. The women were particularly lavish in their praise: "Saul has slain his thousands, and David his ten thousands" (1 Samuel 18:7).

Mind you, the reason David was in the picture at all was that Saul had already been told that his days as king were over. He had disobeyed a clear command of God, and so he was in the process of being stripped of his title in favor of this young man who was described in Scripture as "a man after God's own heart." Saul simply could not accept this public humiliation.

He vented his hostility. "They have ascribed to David ten thousands, but to me they have ascribed thousands. Now what more can he have but the kingdom?" (v. 8). Give him a passing grade for honesty, if not for humility! The comparison stung.

Then here comes the surprise. We read, "Now it came about on the next day that an evil spirit from God came mightily upon Saul, and he raved in the midst of the house, while David was playing the harp with his hand, as usual; and a spear was in Saul's hand" (v. 10). And with that Saul hurls the spear at David, but he escapes.

An "evil spirit from the Lord"!

We might have thought the text should read, "An evil spirit from Satan came mightily upon Saul." But no, this demon was from God. A messenger of Satan became the messenger of God.

Here is a principle you can count on: God always disciplines

His disobedient people by turning them over to the control of their enemies (Deuteronomy 28:47–48). This demon was sent to torment the king by exploiting his jealousy. Little wonder Saul became ever more paranoid, lashing out at David for no particular reason. And even though David's humility would later cause Saul to cry to God in repentance, it proved to be only halfhearted. Saul died a defeated and angry man. He never did know the joy of forgiveness and restoration with God.

The demon was used by God to discipline the rebellious king. If Saul chose to be jealous, then let him be consumed by this vice. If he would not turn to God with his whole heart, then let him serve sin with his whole heart. If he thought that his way was better than submission to God, then let him learn what it is like to be in submission to evil. Let him be driven to despair that he might be driven back into the arms of God.

Let him experience the lies of the devil.

Perhaps now we can understand the interesting story of Ahab and his "lying prophets." When he asked these four hundred men whether he should go up and smite the town of Ramoth-gilead, they gave him the answer he wanted: Yes, he could make an attack and be successful. When Micaiah, the true prophet, was called, he initially gave the same reply, reflecting the wishes of the godless king. The king knew Micaiah was playing a game and finally told him to tell the truth.

Micaiah then gave an honest prophecy: Israel would be scattered like sheep if Ahab attempted to fight the Syrians. As for the four hundred false prophets, Micaiah gave this word from the Lord: God was sitting on His throne and asked for volunteers to entice Ahab to go up and fall at Ramoth-gilead. Various spirits gave different answers, but one spirit volunteered to be a deceiving spirit in the mouth of Ahab's prophets. And God said to him, "You are to entice him and also prevail. Go and do so" (1 Kings 22:22).

Then Micaiah continued, "Now therefore, behold, the Lord has put a deceiving spirit in the mouth of all these your prophets; and the Lord has proclaimed disaster against you" (v. 23). Ahab knew the truth but went into the battle disguised, thinking he could outwit the prophecy of God. But a man drew his bow at random, and the arrow pierced between the pieces of Ahab's armor and he died.

Thus, the Lord put a deceiving spirit in the mouths of the false prophets. The evil spirit who volunteered was given the assignment. Calvin, commenting on this passage, says that God holds Satan with a bridle, and thus the Evil One is "compelled to render Him service wherever God impels him." If God wants to use a demon to tell an evil king a lie, there will be one who will do it. If the Almighty needs more, He will have that also.

You might think that these were examples from the Old Testament, but what about the New? Yes, even today, when we rebel, we choose the scene of the battle, and the Lord might use Satan to discipline us. When Paul chides the church for the careless attitude they had toward sin in their congregation, he tells them that they are a discredit to Christ. As for the immoral man, he should be excommunicated, for "a little leaven leavens the whole lump of dough" (1 Corinthians 5:6).

Paul tells the Corinthians, "I have decided to deliver such a one to Satan for the destruction of his flesh, that his spirit may be saved in the day of the Lord Jesus" (v. 5). Here is a believer who is being given over to the devil! A man who is in the kingdom of light, being made subject to the darkness.

Again, Satan's role is to be the agent of God's discipline. If the man will not submit to the truth of God, let him experience the lies of the devil. If he wishes to live like the pagans, then let him be driven by the god of the pagans. At any rate, Satan will do whatever God wants him to. Nothing less, nothing more.

When Hymenaeus and Alexander made "shipwreck" of the faith, Paul's response was to "hand them over to Satan, so that they will be taught not to blaspheme" (1 Timothy 1:20). The severity of the discipline would, he hoped, bring them to their senses.

You have heard, I'm sure, the honest confession of a Christian who has lived in immorality. I've spoken to more than one such individual who has told me of the torment, rationalizations, guilt, emptiness, and, yes, the harassment of Satan. God wants to make us so miserable that the pain of repentance and restoration will be more bearable than the pain of secrecy and continued rebellion.

We recall David's words before he repented, "For day and night Your hand was heavy upon me; my vitality was drained away as with the fever heat of summer" (Psalm 32:4). Those are the words of a man who knows the torments of God's discipline.

Luther points out that the devil is God's tool, like a hoe that is used to cultivate God's garden. Though the hoe might take pleasure in destroying the weeds, it can never move out of God's hands, nor weed where He does not wish, nor thwart His purpose of building a beautiful garden. Thus the devil always does God's work. Even today, God uses Satan to discipline the disobedient.

GOD USES SATAN TO PURIFY HIS CHOSEN ONES

Then there is the interesting experience of the apostle Paul. He was given a thorn in the flesh, a messenger of Satan to buffet him. This was not because of any sin he committed. It was to prevent Saul from self-exaltation. "Because of the surpassing greatness of the revelations, for this reason, to keep me from exalting myself, there was given me a thorn in the flesh, a messenger of Satan to torment me—to keep me from exalting myself" (2 Corinthians 12:7). Another instance in which God chose the scene of the battle.

After Paul had prayed about it three times, God replied that the thorn would not be removed but that Paul would be given the grace to bear it. To which Paul responded, "Most gladly, therefore, I will rather boast about my weaknesses, that the power of Christ may dwell in me. Therefore I am well content with weaknesses, with insults, with distresses, with persecutions, with difficulties, for Christ's sake; for when I am weak, then I am strong" (vv. 9–10).

Paul said, in effect, "My enemy, this messenger of Satan who means me harm, actually is doing me good." Satan never becomes our friend, for he hates us and seeks our destruction, but he can do us good if he is sent by God to purify us. God uses Satan to show us that God's grace can be sufficient even in the thorns of life.

When Paul was able to accept the thorn in the flesh as a messenger of Satan sent by the Heavenly Father, he was able to see it in an entirely different light. Now he could give thanks for the trial (the thorn). If Satan could act independently of God, such thanks to God would be impossible.

I have noticed in counseling that those Christians who can give thanks to God for their demonic affliction are usually the first to experience the freedom of Christ in their lives. When they begin to see their trials as from the Father of light rather than the father of darkness, they see that there is a larger purpose in it all. Such faith is anathema to the forces of evil.

We should never give thanks to God for sin, or, for that matter, we should never give thanks to God for Satan. But we can give thanks for the way God uses evil to accomplish His purposes. We can give thanks for our own struggles and temptations and say, "Even in this, God is good and His will is being done."

We are in training. Training takes suffering, discipline, faith, and discernment. Even Christ learned obedience by the things that He suffered.

BETWEEN GOD AND THE DEVIL

What implications does God's absolute power over Satan have for counseling? Obviously, we cannot treat every situation alike.

Just imagine Job, Paul, and King Saul at a modern-day deliverance ministry crusade. They would probably be told that all they needed to do was to rebuke Satan, for after all, he is a defeated foe! What might be overlooked is God's purpose in the struggle. Many times believers might be seeking a quick deliverance when God might be seeking a lasting repentance.

God has different purposes in our demonic conflict. For some it is to bring them to repentance; for others it is a means of purification; for others it is for testing in trials. It is both simplistic and wrong to say that we can always rebuke Satan and thus be delivered from his wiles. God might send him to us as surely as he did to Job. What we can say with confidence is that we need not obey Satan's seductions to get us to sin (the subject of another chapter). Deliverance takes discernment.

God and the devil are both involved in our temptations and struggles. We must understand their separate purposes.

1. *We must distinguish between what God wants and what Satan wants.* Satan and God are both actively involved in our temptations, but of course they have radically different purposes.

Whereas God has an ultimately benevolent purpose in every act, the devil's aim is always to destroy. Satan wanted to destroy Job; God wanted to test him.

God seeks our purification and reconciliation. He desires that we be satisfied with Him. He wants us to be content with His revealed will; in a word, He desires our good. His stated goal is to transform us into the image of Christ, to bring many sons into glory. God wants to do something in our hearts that will last forever. His goal is to teach us that sin is destructive and, in contrast, that righteousness is compelling and good.

Satan longs to separate our soul from fellowship with God. He seeks to divide, to destroy. He wants to take God's sheep and scatter them, to get them away from the shepherd. If we are Christians, our souls belong to God, but we can still be defiled. Satan might not be able to own us, but he would like to destroy us.

If we let him, he will disrupt our fellowship, deaden our affection toward God, and fill our lives with sin. That, at least, is his agenda. He wants to trap, to ensnare, and to paralyze. He wants us to become as much like him as possible in his rebellion and independence.

This sets up a perfect environment for us to declare our loyalty to Christ, to side with God's agenda. Only in the flames of temptation and trial are we purified. Remember, everything that God does in our life is to increase our joy, if not in this life, then assuredly in the life to come.

2. *We must distinguish between God's authority and our authority.* The devil has to obey God's every command, but not necessarily *our* every command. Christ is above every principality and power and we are seated with Him in heavenly places (Ephesians 2:6). However, because God has a purpose in Satan's work in the world, you and I do not have absolute authority over the Evil One. We've all heard preachers talk to the devil as if he had to obey their every whim. The Evil One often responds with defiance and, no doubt, gleeful contempt.

Only God has unlimited authority over Satan. In Washington, D.C., a prayer meeting was held in which a man shouted with more enthusiasm than understanding, "I command Satan and his demons to leave Washington, D.C. and never return!" There is, I think, telling evidence that the devil and his demons did not leave Washington. If the Evil One were totally under our power, we would forbid him to work in every city in the world; even better, we would cast him into the abyss. If we were in charge, what short work we would make of him!

On December 13, 1995, Pastor Julio Ruibal was gunned down in Cali, Colombia. He had been especially used by God in the uniting of the churches and in a ministry of prayer. He was in the sixth day of a fast. No one knew better than he the fact that in Christ we are conquerors; no one had more consistently fought against the wiles of the devil and exercised his authority against the devil. But that did not prevent his brutal murder; he, like Christ, suffered martyrdom at the hands of evil men who did Satan's bidding. His death has brought unity and power to the churches he left behind.

If we ask why the devil is still in Colombia, or, for that matter, in Washington, D.C., the answer is that "the Lord hath need of him." The Evil One still has a work to do; there are still assignments he is to carry out. We can do no better than remind ourselves of what Luther said when a pastor friend of his was murdered in 1527. Luther felt deeply about this tragedy and pondered it carefully. It was, he said, the work of an evil person. The evil person was the devil's tool, but the devil was God's tool. Thus the Christian could see even in this the providence of God. God, either in this life or the next, would turn every evil for good.

Here is a verse that summarizes the thrust of this chapter. To the first-century church at Smyrna, Christ said, "Do not fear what you are about to suffer. Behold, the devil is about to cast some of you into prison, so that you will be tested, and you will have tribulation for ten days. Be faithful unto death, and I will give you the crown of life" (Revelation 2:10).

Don't miss this:

- Though this church was persecuted at the hands of the devil, it was still firmly in the hands of God.
- The reason Satan was given authority to cast believers into prison is that they might be tested.
- The length and severity of the testing is determined by Christ. If He says that the testing is to be ten days, even Satan's full fury cannot extend it to *eleven* days!

We have all the authority we need to stand against the devil; we have all the power we need to do God's will, but we do not have absolute control over our enemy. We cannot demolish his kingdom; we cannot prescribe the boundaries of his power. Paul did not think that he always had to duel the devil or take authority over him. He wrote that he wanted to come to Thessalonica, but "Satan thwarted us" (1 Thessalonians 2:18). At times Paul could accept Satan's limitation as God's intervention.

Please don't interpret this to mean that we can stand idly by and watch Satan do his work and simply say, "This is the will of God." We are to be actively fighting the enemy, standing against his assaults. *Indeed, Satan is given to us that we might fight against him.* But it is how we fight that matters. We can fight with more faith and understanding if we know that Satan is always subject to God.

Our war is winnable.

And yet we must give a more detailed answer to this question: What does the Serpent want from us?

8

WHAT THE SERPENT
WANTS FROM YOU

We're in a war.
We can't plead pacifism.
We can't run from the bullets.
We can't hide from the bombs.
We can't plead medical deferment.

If you have never felt the war within, I can't identify. The struggle keeps raging, even after we have walked with God for years. Part of it is the struggle between flesh and spirit; part of it is Satan who harasses us with his ideas and rationalizations and by magnifying our desires. Sins we thought were gone keep cropping up unexpectedly. As one man said, "The devil is now coming to collect for the sins I committed in my youth."

What does the Serpent want from you and me? In short, he wants us to sin that our souls will be separated from God. He wants us to reject God's authority, just as he did, so that we might share his fate. He is angry at God and is particularly annoyed that at least some of the human race will be redeemed. We are the targets of his fury and relentless attacks. All this is to promote his consuming desire: recognition and worship. He wants us to be like him.

If we are believers, he knows he cannot keep us from God's love and that our souls are eternally secure, since we are God's children. The best he can do is to break our fellowship with God; he wants us to become contaminated with sin so that God is obscured. He longs to prove that our loyalty to God is superficial and based on warped motives. If he cannot keep us from heaven, at least he can keep us from usefulness on earth.

What he would really like to do is to prove that he can meet our deepest needs more successfully than God. If we follow him, his argument goes, we can have more potential, fulfillment, and happiness. He will do for us what God cannot. We do not have to humble ourselves to be blessed. There is no need for confession of sin, no need for submission to the Almighty. What we need is to be self-absorbed, self-motivated, and self-driven. This, the Serpent hisses, is what life is really all about.

George Mueller, who is known for having built many orphanages without asking for money, spent many hours in prayer each day. He said that the first duty of every Christian is to find his soul satisfied with God. So Mueller read the Bible each morning and spent time in prayer until his soul was "happy in God," as he put it. This is the happiness Satan will try to sabotage. What he fears most is Christians who have found God to be delightful. He has nothing that can compete.

The question of who was Lord needed to be demonstrated.

His chief method is to make sin look good to us. He does not want us to fear disobedience, but to develop confidence in our ability to control it and its consequences. Sins of all shapes and sizes come wrapped in the most attractive packages. There is something for everyone. He does not explain the law of unintended consequences.

Of course God has His purpose in our testing too. He does

not *tempt* us to lure us to evil (James 1:13), but He does *test* us to give us an opportunity to show how much we love Him. Every temptation that Satan brings our way turns out to be a test of our loyalty to God. If you loved Ford cars, you would want to see them tested to prove their dependability; if you hated Ford cars, you would like to see them tested to prove them deficient. Same test. Different purposes.

God's intention, we are learning, is our refinement, strengthening, and good. But if we don't already know that, temptation can lead to our ruin, to a wasted life, to bondage to sin. That which God can use for maximum good can, if we are not careful, turn out to be for our maximum detriment. The stakes in the conflict are high.

Let us take a walk into the Judean desert and relive the conflict between the Serpent and Christ. Here we see a classic battle, and we can learn from the outcome.

We must grasp the significance of the first verse, "Then Jesus was led up by the Spirit into the wilderness to be tempted by the devil" (Matthew 4:1). Many people think that Christ went into the wilderness so that He would have a place to hide, but alas, the devil found him! The opposite is the case. Christ was driven into the wilderness by the Holy Spirit that He might find the devil to confront him! For thousands of years Christ had listened to the devil's boasts, and now the question of who was Lord needed to be demonstrated. Christ was in the wilderness by the will of God; He was fighting against Satan by the will of God. And, thanks be, He won by the will of God.

God led Christ to be tempted by the devil to *test* Him to prove that He is all wheat. Specifically, God wanted to prove that Christ would win in the very arena of temptation where Adam failed. Satan, on the other hand, turns the test into a *temptation* to try to separate Christ from His Father. The plan was to get Christ to do what Satan himself did in past ages. He wanted Christ to be disqualified as a Savior and, for that matter, to be disqualified as the beloved Son of God.

In previous ages, Lucifer and Christ had often met in the glories of heaven. After Lucifer's plunge into sin, he found it impossible to tempt Christ in the heavens above. But now that "the Word was made flesh," Satan thought he might strike a blow to Christ's humanity. Though Christ, as God, could not sin, Christ might be able to sin as man (at least that must have been what Satan thought). So Satan, with unmitigated audacity, attempts to do what he most surely knew was impossible. *He tries to triumph over the very Christ who created him!*

Christ had just been baptized in the Jordan River; He had just glimpsed into heaven. Now He was to glimpse into hell. Someone has said that He had just seen the dove; now He must see the devil. On the heels of Christ's great spiritual experience, the devil strikes.

THE STRATEGY

Christ, we know, was "tempted in all things as we are" (Hebrews 4:15). That doesn't mean He was tempted to watch sensual movies in a motel room or cheat on his income tax. It does mean that He was tempted through all the avenues that you and I have experienced: the "lust of the flesh and the lust of the eyes and the boastful pride of life" (1 John 2:16). As we walk through this passage, we will be able to identify with Christ at every point, because He so closely has identified with us.

Attempt #1: Turn Away from the Will of God

"If You are the Son of God, command that these stones become bread" (Matthew 4:3). That word *if* should be translated "since." Satan is orthodox in his understanding of who Christ is. He knew Christ was the Son of God. The Evil One's theology on the inspiration of the Bible, the existence of God, and the person of Christ is more accurate than that of theological liberals who deny those truths. The devil believes and trembles, yet he goes on rebelling. He has never found it easy to act on what he knows.

To turn stones into bread was not only possible for Christ, but was the kind of miracle He would later perform. Within a few months He would be standing on the shores of Galilee, taking five loaves and two fish in His hand, and with them feeding a multitude. Christ compassionately met the needs of other people; there would have been nothing wrong with Him meeting His own needs.

Except for this: It was not yet time for Christ to eat. He and His Father had apparently specified when the fast was to be over. To perform a miracle now would be to interfere with the divine plan. As always, Satan took a legitimate need and asked Christ to satisfy it in an illegitimate way. The essence of this temptation was to show that the needs of the body are more important than the needs of the soul. Today is more important than tomorrow. Desires, not duty. Power, not poverty.

Here we come to the subtlety of temptation. If what is presented to us were inherently evil, it would be much easier to resist. We find temptation alluring precisely because the banquet that is spread in our path looks so good; and it looks good because it *is* good—in the right time and the right place.

We think of sexual temptation, which is appealing because it seems so reasonable that our needs should be met. Indeed, hedonists throughout the centuries have reasoned, "When I crave food, I eat; when I desire sex, I find a partner to have it with." Thus the cravings of the body that cry out for fulfillment are satisfied apart from the will of God.

Whether it is sex, food, or pleasure, God has prescribed the rules. He has done so because He wants to see us fulfilled, not because He wants to see us frustrated. Our challenge is to have the faith to believe that His way is best, even when it doesn't appear to be so on the surface. Our assignment, like that of Eve, is to believe that even a good tree will become poison if God has forbidden it.

Christ saw the temptation for what it was. Though ravaged by hunger, He replied, "It is written, 'Man shall not live on bread alone, but on every word that proceeds out of the mouth of God'" (v. 4). The bread that satisfies the soul is more important than that which satisfies the body. Christ appealed to a higher authority and a higher purpose. If the devil would come with error, Christ would combat him with truth.

The devil did not get the *dis*obedience he wanted, but God the Father got the *obedience* He wanted! Thus we see the purpose of temptation: It is to give us a powerful opportunity to declare our loyalty, to show that we believe that God's way is best even when we don't always feel it is so.

Attempt #2: Turn Away from the Word of God

The second temptation is trickier.

If Christ quotes the Scripture, so will the devil. With spectacular power, Satan scoops Christ up and carries Him to Jerusalem and stands Him on the pinnacle of the temple. "The devil took Him into the holy city and had Him stand on the pinnacle of the temple" (v. 5). Of course, the devil could not have done this without Christ's consent. Whether the pinnacle was the apex of the roof of the temple or one of the battlements that overlooks the Kidron Valley, we do not know. What is clear is that Christ actually was brought to the location by demonic power.

"If You are the Son of God, throw Yourself down; for it is written, 'He will command His angels concerning You'; and 'On their hands they will bear You up, so that You will not strike Your foot against a stone'" (Matthew 4:6). What Satan says comes right out of Psalm 91:11–12. Here is the devil, without a copy of the Bible in his hands, quoting verses as if he believed them!

Some writers are at pains to point out that the devil did leave out a crucial phrase in the quotation. The entire verse from the Psalm reads, "He will give His angels charge concerning you, to guard you in all your ways" (Psalm 91:11). The devil omitted that little phrase "in all your ways," skirting around the truth that God will keep us only if we are in His will, walking in the paths He has ordered for us.

Others insist that the omission does not substantially change the meaning of the verse. The devil appears to have been true to the gist of the text. The point is that he does quote Scripture, and he does it to lure Christ into sin!

Let us not miss the point. The devil quotes Scripture for evil motives. By using Scripture he wanted to thwart Christ's ability to quote Scripture. He would wrest the sword of the Spirit from Christ's hands and use it for his own sinister purposes. He uses the Word of God, which should keep us from sin, to provoke Christ into committing a sin. He does it by pitting one passage of Scripture *against* another, rather than putting passages of Scripture *beside* each other. *His desire is to get us to choose to sin even while pointing to a verse in an open Bible.*

The notion that Satan always says evil things is simply not true. He can quote God's Word and even mouth doctrine. He will come as close to the truth as he possibly can in order to deceive, manipulate, and lay a religious trap for his intended victims. Some of his lies are perilously close to the truth.

I met a man who would hear a voice that encouraged him to attend church and be loving. He assumed that this was Christ, because the message was positive and uplifting. But demons will spout good advice. They will speak of unity, quote snatches of Scripture, and encourage good works. All of this to lure the unsuspecting victims into their realm of control.

Don't think for a moment that Satan was trying to drive Christ back to the Bible as a basis for His decisions. This was a deliberate misuse of the Word, so that Christ might be tempted to ignore the Word. The verse was never intended to encourage us to flirt with danger so that we can prove the faithfulness of God. To have danger surprise us is one thing; to seek it so that we can be heroes is another.

Jump, God will catch you!

I saw a preacher on TV who claimed that if people sent him money, God would make them rich. If they had one of his prayer cloths, they would be healed. And if they were to come to one of his meetings, they would have a year's worth of blessings. Devilish presumption.

We can fall into the devil's trap whenever we misinterpret the Word of God and insist that God give us what He has not promised. We can become presumptuous when we refuse to submit our decisions to God, assuming that we ourselves already know what is best. By claiming to use the Word, we can nullify it.

Christ responded with a verse of His own: "On the other hand, it is written, 'You shall not put the Lord your God to the test'" (v. 7). Christ did not have to "test" God as the devil wanted Him to do. Our Lord knew that God was true to His promises if rightly interpreted. He did not fall into the devil's trap of using one verse of Scripture to nullify others. Again He returns to the Word for His authority and power.

The faith by which Christ glorified God was the same faith by which the devil was defeated. So far, Christ has won two out of two. And yet the devil is not finished.

Attempt #3: Turn Away from the Cross

"Again the devil took Him to a very high mountain and showed Him all the kingdoms of the world and their glory; and he said to Him, 'All these things I will give you, if You fall down and worship me'" (vv. 8–9). Once more, Christ is transported by the power of the devil, this time to the top of a very high mountain. The devil showed him all the kingdoms of this world: Imperial Rome with its palaces, ancient Greece with its art, and Egypt with its pyramids. This and more could belong to Christ for a simple and single act of worship.

Satan, knowing that Christ would someday rule the world, was offering Him a shortcut to the kingdom. If He were to bypass the Cross, He could get to the crown with less suffering. So the "god of this world" offers the kingdom to the God of heaven. The usurper tries to make a deal with the owner.

Theologians are divided as to whether the devil had the right to make Christ this offer. Some insist that the world belongs to God and the devil only pretends to own it. It was not his to give away. His title deed to planet Earth is counterfeit.

Others remind us that, yes, God is the owner of the world and all that is in it. However, he has delegated the leadership of the world to Satan. God gave it over into his hands, and perhaps Satan thought he had the right to "give" it back. At any rate, Christ did not challenge his authority to make the offer.

The offer was bold and breathtaking. Lucifer, now turned Satan, who once worshiped Christ in heaven, now tries to get Christ to worship him on earth. He knew that Christ was the rightful King of heaven and earth; he could recall how often they had met on friendly terms in ages past. But now he wants the tables turned. Thirsting as he was for a moment of glory, the Evil One took the gamble. At best, Christ as man might comply; at worst, the Evil One will have to admit defeat again.

Now we can better understand why Christ chided Peter when the apostle suggested that Christ not go to Jerusalem. Peter must have been startled to hear Christ say, "Get behind Me, Satan! You are a stumbling block to Me; for you are not setting your mind on God's interests, but man's" (Matthew 16:23). Of course, Peter didn't realize that by encouraging Christ to cancel Easter, he (Peter) was making a suggestion that would have sealed his own doom. If Christ had not been killed, Peter, along with the rest of us, would have been lost.

But Christ would not turn aside from the will of God. Here in the desert He replied, "Go, Satan! For it is written, 'You shall worship the Lord your God, and serve Him only'" (Matthew

4:10). And so Satan's most coveted desire was left unfulfilled. He knew that if he had been worshiped, he would have to have been obeyed. But since he was not worshiped, he could only go on acting as though he were. He would always have to be satisfied with the fantasy and not the real thing.

Today Satan can no longer tempt Christ to avoid the Cross, but he can tempt us to belittle it. We can cheapen it whenever we think we must do some penance to be forgiven. We so often bear our guilt because we forget that Christ died for all of our sin.

Or we can diminish the Cross by thinking we have committed a sin that is too big for God to forgive. Thus many people think they have committed the "unpardonable sin," not realizing that if they had done so, they would not be troubled about it.

We can also minimize the Cross by thinking that the answer to America's ills lies in politics or moral reform, rather than through the power of the Cross, which is God's only way to reconcile men to Himself.

Every time we diminish the Cross, Satan has accomplished his mission. He wants us to think that there can be a crown without a Cross, salvation without the Substitute. Thus, the conflict between God's will and the "kingdoms of the world" is still going on today.

Christ passed His test; the devil failed his. God was honored because Christ had resolutely declared that He would inherit the kingdom in the Father's way; Satan was dishonored, confined once again to play the role of a loser. Angels came and ministered to Christ. For now the battle was over, but, as we know, the devil would be back at "an opportune time" (Luke 4:13).

CHRIST'S VICTORY TODAY

Today Satan and Christ no longer meet in the wilderness of Judea. Christ is seated in heaven as head of the church at the right hand of God the Father. He has in His possession "the key of David." He describes Himself as "He who is holy, who is true, who has the key of David, who opens and no one will shut, and who shuts and no one opens" (Revelation 3:7). A key represents authority. In His case it is unquestioned, sovereign authority.

The trustees of our church in Chicago issue different keys to different employees. Some keys will just get you into the building;

others will also let you into the office area. Then there is another key that will take you into the building, the office area, and a specific office. Finally, there is the master key that will open any door in the facility, including the closets and the storage areas.

Christ has the master key to the universe. There is no closet on planet Earth that is closed to Him. We do Him no honor when we say that there are countries that are "closed to the gospel." If we think that there is some pocket of resistance that the gospel cannot overcome, we diminish His authority in the world. He has the key to every family and every heart. He also holds the key to our suffering and our struggles with the devil.

One day a minister told me about a town he described as the "occult capital of the Midwest." He said it had more covens, satanic rituals, and demonically controlled individuals per capita than anywhere else. His church was struggling, he said, because the area was "a minister's graveyard." Arsonists tried to burn his church and the members were harassed.

I can appreciate the opposition he was receiving, but I have some good news for him. I know of a church next to a nest of satanically induced worshipers and yet the church flourished because of the direct intervention of Christ. This was the church in Philadelphia, situated along the seacoast in Asia minor.

Because He has the key of David, Christ could say to this church, "Behold, I have put before you an open door which no one can shut. . . . Behold, I will cause those of the synagogue of Satan, who say that they are Jews and are not, but lie—I will make them to come and bow down at your feet, and make them know that I have loved you" (Revelation 3:8–9). We might be tempted to think that Satan had the key to this synagogue; after all, it was dominated by his authority and power. But Christ can override the Evil One and assure the church that these Jews will become believers; the followers of Satan will become the followers of Christ.

Satan's key to this synagogue will only get him so far. Christ has the master key. Or better, Satan only pretends to have the key, deluding others to think that he is the one who can shut doors and open them. Fact is, he can do neither; he can neither open nor shut a door but that Christ wills it so. Thus Christ our Lord can say that He has opened a door that no one can close and "will cause those of the synagogue of Satan . . . to bow at your feet." Satan's grip is gone, and all that he can do is whimper while Christ wins.

Christ alone has the key to heaven and hell, the key to Moroc-co and Japan, the key to Germany and France. Christ alone has the key to "the occult capital of the Midwest." And if Christ wish-es to open a door, no one can shut it; and if He chooses to close a door, no one can open it! Sometimes, as Paul knew, Christ will open a door but leave many adversaries (1 Corinthians 16:9). Yet he also knew that if Satan appeared personally with every one of his enraged demons, the entire troupe would have to humbly submit to the One with the key to the universe in His hands!

If a door is closed, then let us boldly affirm that Christ has willed it closed for reasons unknown to us. Let us with equal boldness affirm that there is no door that Christ cannot open. When Paul was in prison, he encouraged the believers at Colosse to pray for him "that God will open up to us a door for the word, so that we may speak forth the mystery of Christ, for which I have also been imprisoned" (Colossians 4:3). Closed doors are often given to us that our faith and persistence might be tested. But there would be little use of praying and striving to see them opened if Satan had the power to keep them closed. And so we now ask: What does the devil want from us?

And what does God want to see happen in our lives?

SATAN'S PURPOSES/GOD'S PURPOSES

We also have our wilderness. James writes that we are tempt-ed when we are carried away and enticed by our own lust. Then he adds, "Then when lust has conceived, it gives birth to sin; and when sin is accomplished, it brings forth death" (James 1:15). Our greatest challenge is to do what we know to be right; it is to believe that sin is as bad as God says it is, and that Satan, for all of his alluring power, in the end will deceive us.

What Does Satan Want?

Sometimes demonic temptations take an extreme form. Here is a part of a letter I received from someone who is experiencing her own Judean wilderness. The attacks are relentless and ongoing.

I've been a Christian for ten years and every one of those years has been characterized by heavy demonic attack. I have the dubious gift

of being in tune with the spirit world because of my previous involvement in the occult. Evil spirits talk to me all day long, using obsceni-
ties and harassment. Although I can see them clearly, my husband
cannot. I have experienced sexual attacks, fear, and insomnia.

I have grown incredibly angry, even at God because I cannot
understand why God would allow a Christian to undergo such terrible trials for so long. I assumed that there was some terrible sin in
my life, but apparently this is not the case. Although God is giving
me the grace to handle these trials, I am becoming withdrawn.

Anyone who has written or spoken on the subject of Satan
has heard heart-wrenching stories of those who are bound by
our enemy. Because he knows us so well, his attacks against us
suit us exactly. He exploits our weaknesses and persists with his
suggestions. In the case of some, they are harassed by demonic
afflictions.

This is not the place to try to analyze this troubled woman's
plight in detail, but some things jump out at us from the letter.

First, Satan wants this lady to turn away from God, to get her
to believe that God is simply either unable to meet her needs or
else is disinterested in her plight. And if God doesn't care for her,
then she must care for herself. Satan is a thief, so he comes to
steal her joy.

Second, Satan wants to dominate, to take back the control of
this woman's life. If she were to follow his suggestions, she would
experience even greater pressure to take her disobedience to its
logical conclusion. The Serpent wants to become her suitor, her
companion as she walks through life. He makes changing the
direction of her life look impossible. Despair is the devil's most
persistent weapon.

Third, and this is implied, Satan would like to have her discredit her testimony, to have her witness to God's inability to take
care of His own children. When David committed murder and
adultery, the Lord said that news of what he had done had "given
occasion to the enemies of the Lord to blaspheme" (2 Samuel
12:14). The people of God are Satan's most coveted trophy. He
knows that God will have them in heaven forever. His only
opportunity to harass them is now. He is an accuser who would
like to discredit this woman.

The final step, of course, is that Satan wants her to look to
him to do what God is apparently not willing to do. When we are

in a tight place with no end to our suffering in sight, it is then that we are most apt to turn away from God.

Satan evidently wants to wear this woman down, that she might collapse in despair. Reread the letter to feel her near hopelessness as she becomes angry at God because of the long struggle. Since we cannot win these battles without faith, the enemy seeks to make us weary, feeling that the fight is not worth it. Despair drives faith from our hearts.

So much for what he wants!

What Does God Want?

There is no easy answer for those who are harassed by Satan, but there is an answer. But first we must try to think of what God wants to have happen in the midst of the conflict.

If Satan wants to *pulverize* us, God wants to *purify* us. God wants us to declare our loyalty to Him. We cannot say that we love God with all of our mind, heart, and soul unless we are willing to make some difficult choices in His favor. We can only prove our love for God when we say *Yes!* to him when all of the passions of our body and soul are screaming *No!*

God is also glorified when we believe that the truth of His Word is stronger than the error of Satan's lies. God wants some people who will actually believe Him when He says that there is more happiness to be found in Him than there is to be found in the world. *Blessed is the person who believes in God despite the fact that every inch is contested.*

God's second purpose is to reveal Himself to us, to come to us in renewed love and understanding. It is when we have confronted the devil and won that we can expect God to minister to us, just as angels ministered to Christ. God wants us to be convinced of His greatness and glory so that we will never again give Satan the power he wishes to wield over us.

Abraham faced the most excruciating temptation in history when he was asked to offer Isaac on the altar. We know that Abraham passed the test, even believing that, if necessary, God would raise Isaac from the dead in order that God's promise might be fulfilled. As he left the mountain, bless him, he marked the spot by calling it "Jehovah-jireh," that is, "The Lord Will Provide." Just think of the fresh ideas of God that flooded his soul.

From this point on, he would worship differently, he would serve differently, and later he would die differently. The Abraham who came down from the mountain was a different man than the Abraham who went up that mountain. He was transformed by the temptation because he endured it successfully.

To return to the letter: We should not overlook what God might be saying to this woman's Christian friends. When Paul wrote in Ephesians that we should above all take "the shield of faith with which you will be able to extinguish all the flaming missiles of the Evil One," he knew that this is one piece of armor we just cannot live without. Apparently in those days the shields were beveled, that is, made with an edge that would allow them to interlock. Thus when an army marched into battle, it appeared as if a long wall were moving right into the camp of the enemy.

There are some battles we cannot fight alone. That is why Paul wrote, "The eye cannot say to the hand, 'I have no need of you'; or again the head to the feet, 'I have no need of you'" (1 Corinthians 12:21). There are times when the body of Christ must rally behind one of its weakest members. If Satan wished to wear this woman down, the body must wear him down through intercession, the ministry of the Word, and counseling.

We must come alongside those who have become exhausted in the battle. When we cannot pray for ourselves, we must have others pray for us. God is faithful, not just when we win, but when we fight and there is no permanent victory. If we remember that the devil is under His supervision, we will believe that God has a purpose in deepening our walk with Him even while the struggle rages.

No matter Satan's motivation, God's purpose toward His children is always benevolent. We do not have to see instant deliverance in order for God to be glorified. We just need to affirm that we are never given more than we can bear; we just need to know that we suffer under God's faithful care.

To all who suffer from Satan's continued attacks, we must say, "No temptation has overtaken you but such as is common to man; and God is faithful, who will not allow you to be tempted beyond what you are able, but with the temptation will provide the way of escape also, that you may be able to endure it" (1 Corinthians 10:13). Someone else, somewhere, endured the same affliction that we are experiencing and did so victoriously. Any new trial is an old trial happening to a new person.

Sometimes God teaches us more while we suffer in temptation than we can learn when we are free from it. We are blessed when we can still see the face of God even when a demon speaks in our ears. Of course, we should never be satisfied until the devil flees, though we must also remember that God has His timetable.

Blessed are those who believe God is good even when He doesn't appear to do what we think He should. Here are some words of encouragement from one man who was under satanic attack for what appeared to be a long time—far too long.

> *But He knows the way I take; when He has tried me, I shall come forth as gold. My foot has held fast to His path; I have kept His way and not turned aside. I have not departed from the command of His lips; I have treasured the words of His mouth more than my necessary food.* (Job 23:10–12)

No trial is wasted if God gets what He longs for. God, remember, wins even when He appears to lose; Satan loses even when he appears to win.

9

CLOSING THE DOOR
WHEN THE SERPENT KNOCKS

A con artist worked like this. He could contact a prospective client, assuring the man that a few hundred dollars invested in a specific business venture would double in a matter of months.

The client was leery, but the sales pitch was so impressive that he decided to try it with a modest amount of money. A few hundred dollars was not much to lose.

A few months later, the con man made good on his promise. He returned with a check that doubled the man's money. His extravagant claims appeared to be true.

A month later, the con man returned with a similar promise. This time the investment was a few thousand dollars. Once again, the investor returned an impressive dividend.

So it went. With each encounter, the client developed more confidence in his broker; each time the amount of money increased substantially.

Finally, the satisfied client was willing to give his friend $50,000 with the promise of still higher profits.

With that, the broker disappeared.

Scam operators will tell you to follow some basic nonnegotiable rules if you want to deceive the public.

1. Never lose sight of your long-term goal—the enslavement of your prospects.

2. Think of ways to help your client develop confidence in you. Do nothing to arouse suspicion or fear.

3. Use bait that will appeal to your customer, but be sure to keep the hook skillfully hidden.

4. Make promises that prove the personal benefits of your product. Keep as many promises as possible.

5. Have as many lures as there are interests among the masses. There is no limit to the number of doors that can lead to the final goal of control and entrapment.

Satan has a master plan to deceive the nations of the world. He hopes to redefine our definition of God so that we are willing to switch our allegiances. The Evil One wants us to end up worshipping him rather than the living and true God.

But he also has a personal plan for your life. He has a niche for you in his overall scheme. He believes that he can get us to follow him, at least for a part of our journey. He plants seeds that he hopes will germinate years later. He stays out of view, waiting for that special moment. He knows that he himself is abhorrent to us, so he comes in different disguises, using different names and different interests.

I believe that Christ taught that we all have guardian angels, or that at least children do (Matthew 18:10). Since Satan has set up his rival kingdom to mimic the true kingdom of God, there is reason to think that a demon would be assigned to each of us, to observe us, trying to use each opportunity to lure us into sin. This "guardian angel" would much like to lead us into ruin.

Just as most American soldiers fighting in Europe during World War II had no direct contact with Hitler, but with his underlings, so we seldom, if ever, confront Satan personally. He cannot be in two places at the same time, so he likely maintains a presence at only the most strategic battles. But his many minions are spread throughout the earth. These lesser spirits have varying degrees of intelligence and power. They are highly organized and have been recruited to become his mercenaries, servants who do his bidding. If they disobey, they are likely punished by their cruel tyrant.

Of special interest is our secret life, those attitudes and behaviors we keep from others. Evil spirits quite probably are not able to read the minds of believers, but they observe our actions. They see what we watch on TV; they observe what we read; and, above all, they notice what we say. This provides them with their most fruitful areas of temptation.

His method is to make sin look good to us.

Hunters study animals to become familiar with their likes and dislikes, habits, and environment. They lure animals into circumstances that look attractive but conceal a deadly hook. A trap has the advantage of standing in for the trapper. He does not even have to be there, and the unsuspecting bear can be caught.

If you are catching a mouse, you use cheese; a bear will be drawn to a piece of fresh meat; for fish, you use worms. The trick, of course, is to tempt your prey with what it wants to have, but end up giving it what *you* want it to have.

I believe that Satan has already made meticulous plans for our downfall. All that is left for us to do is to step into the trap that has been carefully laid. Of course, we don't know where the trap is, nor can we see it, but it is there nonetheless.

If we could know the extent of his knowledge about us, if we could understand his fiendish delight should we become a discredit to Christ, we would pore over the Scriptures to learn about him and the kinds of traps that might be laid for us.

Three principles must be remembered. First, Satan is very angry. He is angry at God because he knows that God will win the battle. He is angry because he wants to be like the Most High and yet knows he never will be! He is deeply resentful of God's generosity toward us because he hoped that the entire human race would side with him in his rebellion. To attack us is to get back at God. He is angry when he sees the image of Christ in us.

Second, his method is to make sin look good to us. Whatever

the lure he employs, he wants us to develop confidence in our ability to handle the consequences of disobedience. He will never remind us of the law of unintended consequences.

Third, he works through the sins of the flesh. He takes the sins we already struggle with and strengthens their power. His goal is that he might have a measure of leverage, influencing our lives. He wants Christ evil spoken of; he wants us to stumble so that our lives will be discredited. Since he has no moral scruples, he will do whatever he can to attack us. Nothing is beneath his dignity.

What does he want from us? Control. He wants the privilege of managing our lives. He wants a piece of the action.

STAGES OF CONTROL

Temptation

The first level of control is temptation. Satan, or one of his demons, injects thoughts into our minds which we think are our own. This enables him to remain hidden while luring us into sin. This is brilliant strategy, for even though sin is attractive to us, he is not.

One day a couple decided to sell a piece of property and give some of the proceeds to the church. So far, so good. But they also agreed to pretend that they were contributing *all* of the money they had received. Like many of us, they wanted to appear to be better Christians than they really were. The apostle Peter rebuked them and asked the husband, "Ananias, why has Satan filled your heart to lie to the Holy Spirit and to keep back some of the price of the land?" (Acts 5:3). The man was smitten to death by God because of this sin, and moments later his wife suffered the same fate.

Now, if someone had told them that an evil spirit had put the hypocritical lie into their minds, they would have been surprised. They thought that the idea was their very own. But it was the Evil One who had planted the suggestion in their minds.

Though Satan evidently could not read their thoughts, he was able to inject ideas into their minds. Remember, our minds are spiritual, not physical, substances. It would be incorrect to say, "I had a thought that was about one-third of an inch long and that weighed a half gram!" Our thoughts exist in a realm accessible to the spirit world. That explains why those who pursue mind-expanding techniques or transcendental meditation discover they are in contact with demons. As spiritual beings we can be connected to the spirit world.

The point here, of course, is that Satan can tempt us by giving us ideas. Whether we act on them, however, is ultimately our choice, not his. Ananias and Sapphira acted on the suggestion and paid the consequences.

Obsession

A second stage is oppression or obsession. Recently I spoke to a fine Christian woman who told me that several months ago she began having frightful thoughts. Specifically, she visualized taking a knife to kill her grandchild, who was a few months old. This woman was obsessed with this gruesome prospect.

Interestingly, while she was rearing her own children she had had no such thoughts. Only in recent months, and for no apparent reason, did she now struggle with the fear that she could not be with her grandchild alone. She dreaded that she might act on these fantasies.

Were these ideas her own? I don't think so. How could a loving Christian think of killing her own grandchild whom she adored? The thoughts had their origin with a demonic spirit who, for whatever reason, had come to harass her.

When I assured her that these were not her thoughts, she felt relieved for two reasons. First, she was not the evil woman she had begun to think she was; and second, she now knew that these images need not have power over her. A demon might suggest evil but could not force her to carry it out. In other words, she was in control, whether she realized it or not. She could rebuke the thoughts in the name of Christ with complete confidence that she need not follow the suggestions. Christ was on her side.

Sexual temptation is common to us all. And, I might add, we would have such temptations even if Satan and his demons did not exist. We are, after all, fallen creatures who struggle with sinful lusts and desires. But if we give ourselves to those sins, we give Satan a foothold, an opportunity to return to claim the ground he wants to think is his. I have counseled people who are obsessed with fantasies of sexuality, often depraved and perverted. These thoughts might come while they are singing a hymn in church or trying to pray. The obsessions take priority over all other thoughts. Satan has pulled the noose one notch tighter.

Possession

Third, there is possession. The characteristics of this level of control are most clearly seen in Mark chapter 5. Here a demon not only harasses a man, but actually inhabits his body. We sympathize with this man in his drivenness, in his compulsion to live alone and disfigure his body. Perhaps the reason he was gnashing himself with stones was that he was suicidal. Christ liberated him from those awful powers so that he was clothed and "in his right mind."

Can Christians be possessed? That question is debated today, and the answer might not be entirely clear. Part of the problem is one of terminology. Surely we would all agree that a demon cannot possess a Christian in the sense of owning him or having a direct indwelling as does the Holy Spirit. But some insist that a Christian can be "demonized," that is, have a deep level of demonic involvement even from within the body. The second difficulty in answering the question is that we do not know enough about the human psyche to know exactly where the line between oppression and possession should be drawn.

What seems clear is that there are Christians whose vocal cords have been under the control of a demonic spirit (this might, however, be a possible phenomenon without actual possession as found in the New Testament). I have had encounters with demonic spirits who spoke through the lips of Christians who were under deep demonic oppression. Many other counselors, more knowledgeable than I, have had similar experiences.

Perhaps demons can have a greater level of control over Christians than many of us were taught to believe. But we must always compare Satan's power to God's power, lest we give the Evil One more leverage than he deserves. Our rallying cry must be: "You are from God, little children, and have overcome them; because greater is He who is in you than he who is in the world" (1 John 4:4).

Satan is subject to God, but God does allow him to take us

through the suffering of temptation. Even the ordinary trials of life can become an occasion for temptation. We can't say it too often: We must be alert for the dangers that lie in our path.

SEVEN DOORS

In previous chapters we have learned that God, as in the case of Job, chooses the scene of the battle; sometimes Satan, as in the case of Peter, chooses where the fight will break out. Sometimes we choose our own battlefield, and when we do, it is always to our detriment.

Here are some doors the devil hopes we will open, if just a crack. I do not mean that if we open these doors Satan will come in to indwell us, but rather these are the doors that give him occasion to develop a stronghold, that is, a pattern of sinful behavior that enables him to exert influence over us. He will be back to knock on the door that has once opened to his influence.

There might be other entry points other than those listed here. These are just some of the most obvious, the ones that we are most likely to identify. Stay with me because I will then discuss how we can close these doors and keep them closed.

Rebellion/Self-will

Since the first sin that ever was committed was rebellion, this sin must be listed first. Children who rebel against parental authority, even if it is lovingly administered, or adults who refuse to submit to Christ and to church leadership—these and a dozen other kinds of rebellion delight the Evil One. The "look out for number one" philosophy did not originate in the human mind but was first embraced by Lucifer when he substituted his will for God's.

Rebellion is like the sin of witchcraft, and insubordination is like idolatry (1 Samuel 15:23). The rebellion of drugs, hard rock music, and violence all play in concert with the devil's tune. So does the rebellion of indifference and the rebellion of withdrawal from God and His people. No matter how polite the refusal, when we will not have God to rule over us, we rebel against Him.

Since self-will is at the root of all of our sins, I shall be explaining it more fully in the next chapter. For now, it is enough to remember that man's rebellion is just as detestable to God as Satan's. To rebel is to follow the Prince of Rebels.

Anger

A sign of demonic activity is irrational, uncontrollable anger. Fits of temper often erupt with little or no provocation. Paul wrote, "Be angry, and yet do not sin; do not let the sun go down on your anger, and do not give the devil an opportunity" (Ephesians 4:26–27). The Greek word for opportunity is *topos*, which means "foothold." Anger, like other sins, allows an evil spirit to gain at least a partial entry into one's life. That wedge in the door can become the basis for further anger and demonic exploitation.

One man told me that when his wife became angry, even without provocation, she would be "transformed into another person." She seemed seized by a power that was beyond her, a power that made her brood for days. Of course there might be many hidden reasons for her anger, but simmering anger gives rise to the devil's work.

Men who are angry, often violently and irrationally, devastate their marriages and their children. Even if they should ask forgiveness, damage is done that cannot be repaired. Since anger destroys, the destroyer uses it to further his agenda.

Hatred/Murder

Following on the heels of anger is violence, the expression of hatred and uncontrolled rage. We have already learned that Cain, who killed his brother, did so because he was "of the Evil One" (1 John 3:12). John affirms that one who does not love his brother is acting like a child of the devil. In contrast, the children of God love one another. And then John adds this startling comment: "Everyone who hates his brother is a murderer; and you know that no murderer has eternal life abiding in him" (1 John 3:15). That explains why some who are under the influence of evil spirits desire to "get even" by murder, or for that matter, seek to commit suicide. The devil instigates violence and murder. Christians who commit suicide die defeated, but I believe they will arrive safely in heaven.

Since, as John says, "the whole world lies in the power of the

Evil One" (1 John 5:19), we should not be surprised at the brutality that has existed on this planet from the beginning of creation. An hour of television will confirm that Satan is the god of this age.

Guilt

The name *Adversary* means "Accuser." We've already commented on the vision of Zechariah the prophet, who saw Joshua the high priest standing before the Lord, clothed in filthy garments, symbolizing the sins of the nation. Satan was present too, standing at his right hand "to accuse him." But God took the filthy garments from Joshua and clothed him with festal robes (Zechariah 3:1–7).

Whereas the Holy Spirit uses guilt to drive us to Christ for forgiveness, Satan uses guilt to drive a wedge between God and us. He accomplishes this by making us think that our sins are too great for God to forgive or by making us feel condemned for sins that have already been forgiven.

Satan lies not only with words but with emotions. He attempts to create feelings that alienate us from God, from others, and even from ourselves. He finds it most helpful if we brood in isolation and believe our most painful depressions reflect reality.

Don't let the irony escape you: Satan entices us to sin, and then when we follow his suggestions, he heaps condemnation upon our consciences. He accuses us for the very sins he entices us to commit. How quickly he changes from *tempter* to *accuser!*

Satan's work of accusation will eventually come to an end. "Now the salvation, and the power, and the kingdom of our God and the authority of His Christ have come, for the accuser of our brethren has been thrown down, he who accuses them before our God day and night" (Revelation 12:10).

Along with guilt is a feeling of hopelessness that drives many people to despair. The man possessed by demons lived alone among the tombs (Mark 5:3). He had severed his social relationships, perhaps by choice, or perhaps this was a decision that was made for him by others. At any rate, he became a loner, someone who had withdrawn into his own world of inner torment and fear. Although he was not a believer in Christ until they met and he experienced a glorious deliverance, the same feelings of despair can exist in a believer.

Hopelessness is one of Satan's most believable lies. It has been said that we can live forty days without food, three days without water, and four minutes without air, but we cannot live a minute without hope. The devil knows that hopelessness can only survive without the promises of God. Therefore, the hopelessness becomes helplessness.

False Religions

Satan inspires people to veer off into false cults that dethrone Christ. He leads people into strange occult doctrines. "But the Spirit explicitly says that in later times some will fall away from the faith, paying attention to deceitful spirits and doctrines of demons" (1 Timothy 4:1).

These doctrines might range from asceticism to theoretical speculations about the spirit world. Paul said that when the heathens offer sacrifices to their gods, "they sacrifice to demons and not to God; and I do not want you to become sharers in demons. You cannot drink the cup of the Lord and the cup of demons; you cannot partake of the table of the Lord and the table of demons" (1 Corinthians 10:20–21).

In Deuteronomy 18:9–12, God lists various heathen practices that are an abomination. These include child abuse, divination, witchcraft, omens, sorcery, curses, mediums, seances, and the like. These are all satanic counterfeits instigated to take the place of the true God. There are, of course, many other forms of occultism, many of them associated with mystical Eastern religions.

Fear

The fear of witnessing for Christ, which all of us have experienced, is so natural that we seldom think that Satan would have anything to do with it. Yet, interestingly, before Peter denied that he knew the Savior, Christ explained, "Simon, Simon, behold, Satan has demanded permission to sift you like wheat; but I have prayed for you, that your faith may not fail; and you, when once you have turned again, strengthen your brothers" (Luke 22:31–32).

Many fears are natural and actually helpful to our survival. We should fear driving too fast or crossing the streets without looking. The fear of being mugged reminds us to be careful at night. We all fear sickness, poverty, and death. Frightening child-hood experiences can lead to irrational fears.

But there are those fears that are exaggerated, paralyzing, and controlling. We do not have to be paranoid to be bound by fears that simply are unwarranted. Or, for that matter, there are fears that might be real enough, but they do not need to control us. Christ, for example, said that we need not even fear those who destroy the body, but rather are to "fear Him who is able to destroy both soul and body in hell" (Matthew 10:28).

Fear paralyzes those who give themselves to it. John wrote, "Fear involves punishment, and the one who fears is not perfect-ed in love" (1 John 4:18). If we really feared God, we would have to fear little else.

Sexual Immorality and Perversions

When Paul counseled married couples about their sexual practices, he said that they should not live celibate unless it is for a short time, and in agreement, "so that Satan will not tempt you because of your lack of self-control" (1 Corinthians 7:5).

It is easier to defend a military target than it is to recapture it.

Those who give themselves to immorality soon discover that they are slaves to their passions. Talk to those whom we now call sex addicts and they will tell you about the power of sensual spir-its that drive them on in their endless quest for fulfillment. Pornography, homosexuality, and various other forms of sexual impurity are the devil's playground.

Obviously all of these sins would exist even if Satan were no longer active in the world, for they find their root in the flesh, our fallen nature. But Satan stands by to work through our nature to exploit, magnify, tempt, and destroy.

Since the Scriptures are clear that we must resist the devil, we have to know how to combat him. As Christ warned, "Keep watching and praying, that you may not come into temptation; the spirit is willing, but the flesh is weak" (Mark 14:38).

CLOSING THE DOORS

Luther said that when the devil came knocking on the door of his heart, he would send the Lord Jesus to the door. Christ would say, "Martin Luther used to live here but has moved out. . . . I now live here." Then, says Luther, when the devil would see the nail prints on Christ's hands and His pierced side, he would take flight immediately!

We must keep the door closed, no matter how loudly we hear the knock. Whenever we open the door, we have the tendency to open it even wider the next time. In any battle it is easier to defend a military target than it is to recapture it once it has been in enemy hands.

Interestingly, whatever Satan's role in our temptation might be, the fact is that God holds us accountable for what we do. We are never given the luxury of blaming Satan and evading personal responsibility. We must learn to say no to the devil, just as Christ did. Here are some ways to keep the door bolted.

1. *We must pause and give thanks to God for our test.* This might seem difficult, but our faith will be strengthened when we see our struggles coming from our heavenly Father. God, let us never forget, does the testing and Satan does the tempting. If we cannot thank God we have not yet seen His purpose in it all. We don't give thanks for our sin; we don't give thanks for the devil; but we can give thanks that God has found us to be worthy of being tested.

Our praise must include the assurance that Christ has completely triumphed over the demonic world. We do not fight from the standpoint of weakness, but from the standpoint of strength. Unquestionably, Satan has been crushed. So we give thanks for our struggle. We also give thanks that Christ is high above all principalities and powers. We give thanks that we have been found worthy to suffer this temptation for Christ's sake.

2. *We must learn the meaning of the word "resist."* Most of us think that victory over Satan should come easily. We evoke the

name of Christ, recite a verse of Scripture, and assume that the temptation should leave us. We believe that our desires should subside, our anger dissipate, and we will be content with our surroundings. Jealousy should turn to joy, lust to love, and hatred to holiness—all because we have breathed a prayer.

Peter wrote that Satan was like a roaring lion, stalking about seeking whom he may "devour," and that we were to "resist him" (1 Peter 5:8–9). James repeated the same challenge when he wrote that if we submitted ourselves to God and resisted the devil, he would flee (James 4:7). But neither of those writers believed that we would need to resist only once, or only for short periods of time. Christ resisted, but Satan returned with a greater assault.

For Paul, temptation was war; it was a matter of life and death. He knew there would be casualties. "Put on the full armor of God, so that you will be able to stand firm against the schemes of the devil" (Ephesians 6:11). Standing on the territory that Christ conquered would be exceedingly difficult. Just as Joshua was given the land, but had to fight for it, sometimes winning and sometimes losing, so our inheritance can only be secured with great effort.

Think of the drug addict resisting another fix; think of the pornography addict resisting renting a sensual video; think of the angry husband resisting the impulse to lash out with words and perhaps blows; think of the employer about to be evicted, resisting a much-needed bribe; think of big money waved in your face. In these and other instances, resisting involves self-control and suffering. It is to such affliction that we are called.

It is, however, *how* we resist that makes all the difference. We do not merely stand against these untamed impulses with grit and determination. Rather, we stand against them by looking to God and asking Him to deliver us. We do not look at the evil, for we shall be seduced by it. Rather, we look to Christ, claiming His promises and affirming that we can cope with our distress because we are not enduring it alone. We recite Scripture and we sing hymns, for we know how desperately we have to remain focused on God.

When it comes to sexual passions, for example, we must say with William Gurnall, "Watch over them as one who dwells in a thatched roof house is careful to watch over the sparks that fly out of his chimney for fear that one should land on the thatch and set the whole house on fire." We must resist the first impulse to sin, remembering that saying no will never become easier once the temptation is allowed to lodge in our souls. We must stand against all odds.

Why did Paul say, "Above all, taking the shield of faith"? He said that because if we don't believe in God's availability to help, the devil will pay no attention to our protests. When we conclude that God cannot rescue us, Gurnall again writes, then faith has been lost and "your soul will fall at Satan's feet, too disheartened to keep the door shut any longer to temptation. Remember this: The one who abandons faith in the midst of spiritual drought can be compared to the fool who throws away his pitcher the first day the well is dry."

3. *We must be convinced that sin is always our enemy.* One single act of disobedience can trap us. The mouse usually does not have the luxury of having a series of experiences with traps before it is caught. Just once might be enough.

One act of immorality, one drink of alcohol, or one experiment with drugs just might trigger a roller coaster of experiences where the noose always becomes a bit tighter. And, for such reasons, the resistance must become fiercer. Repentance is always the major requirement of deliverance.

4. *We must use the Scripture against Satan just as Christ did.* We, too, must be able to say to Satan, "Go! for it is written. . . ." Such concentration blocks Satan's attempts to confuse us with his lies. The Word not only cleanses us, but also protects us. Christ said, "You are already clean because of the word which I have spoken unto you" (John 15:3).

I must warn, however, that Satan does not always flee just because Scripture is used against him. Remember that when Christ quoted Scripture Satan came back with another temptation and even quoted a verse of his own.

Unless we are under the authority of God, we cannot exercise His authority. Recall that the sons of Sceva tried to use the name of Jesus, and a demon tore off their clothes and they fled naked (Acts 19:14–16). The Word of God has power for us only when we are submissive to it. And only when we insist on its truth in the face of a challenge will it cause the enemy to flee. Satan leaves when he can no longer get us to believe a lie.

We must quote Scripture often, even when the resistance heightens. We must stay with truth no matter how many grenades are lobbed in our direction. There are times when the temptations are so overwhelming that we must wholeheartedly find our refuge in God. Such victories are the most precious to Him.

Unfortunately, we often say *maybe* rather than *no*, so that we leave the option open to eventually say *yes*. We are like the person trying to get rid of a pesky salesman without saying a firm *no* and closing the door. Though we might protest that we are not interested in buying Satan's products, we leave the door ajar, continuing to discuss his enticements. As long as the matter is under discussion, we leave open the possibility that the devil will make a sale.

Satan will leave off if the door simply will not budge. That does not mean that the battle is over. Indwelling sin, which "doth so easily beset us," is ever with us. Even those who think they have conquered the flesh discover its unpredictable power to tempt, confuse, and subdue. No wonder Christ said, "Keep watching and praying that you may not come to temptation" (Mark 14:38).

Christ taught His disciples to pray, "Lead us not into temptation but deliver us from evil." We should pray, "Lord, when I have the desire to sin, might I not have the opportunity; and when I have the opportunity, might I not have the desire." When we are tried, we shall be like gold.

Several excellent books have been written to help believers combat Satan in the trenches of spiritual warfare. Two I would recommend are *The Adversary*, by Mark Bubeck, and *Reclaiming Surrendered Ground*, by Jim Logan, both published by Moody Press. Often counseling is need to help those who have fallen into addictions, attitudes, and difficulties that need special counsel and instruction.

Our battle is not yet over. We must pinpoint more carefully the root of our struggles. With God's help, we must confess that we sometimes reflect Christ in our lives, but we also can still reflect the devil. We are, after all, creatures who are poised on the brink of eternity. Until then, our struggles continue.

The poison of the Serpent must be neutralized.

10

NEUTRALIZING THE SERPENT'S POISON

Would you be offended if I were to say that we have some of the same characteristics as the devil? We should not be surprised if we do, for a little drop of his rebellion has fallen on every human heart. We may no longer belong to the devil, but sometimes we act like him.

Of course, as believers we also have the characteristics of Christ. God's express purpose in saving us is to make us more like Himself; we are to be His sons and daughters. We are involved in a conflict: We are poised between God and the devil, each desiring our loyalty, each wishing to turn us into his likeness.

Laura had the uncanny ability of being able to take friends and turn them against each other and against her. She was filled with bitterness and refused to submit to authority. Her attitude was understandable, for she had experienced betrayal and abuse. Yet though it was understandable, it was inexcusable. As a Christian she simply did not have to behave as she did. In her confusion, she both sought help and rejected it.

There was no doubt in my mind or hers that she was a Christian, though she also was aware that she was under the influence of an evil presence. Sometimes a demon would speak out of her mouth. This spiritual creature, who always referred to Laura in the third person, would taunt me, challenge me, and ridicule my efforts in counseling her. My best efforts were to no avail.

One Sunday after I had preached, Laura came to me and said, "Pastor, I have hated you ever since you have come to the church—and I am here to apologize and to make things right."

I asked her what I had done to make her so angry, and she said, "Nothing. It is not your fault; it's just that I have bitterness within my heart." Of course I forgave her.

About a month or two later, she called me at home at about eleven o'clock to say that she had been battling demons all evening and was calling to say that she was now free. I told her I would pray with her on the telephone so that she could have a good night of sleep.

As I began to pray, a demonic spirit began to speak through her vocal cords, taunting, "Why did Laura call you so late at night? I want to wear you down." Then he added, "I have caused her to hate you so that she would not hear a word you say at Moody Church." I asked the spirit to identify himself in the name of Christ. He replied, "Love." I said, "Will that stand as truth in the sight of God?" And he said, "No."

After about fifteen minutes of this kind of banter, I rebuked the spirit and talked to Laura. I asked if she knew what had been going on and she said, "Yes . . . I know that a spirit is speaking through me." And yes, she knew what he had been saying.

I prayed with Laura, and that was the last I heard from her. I learned she had left the church, and I assumed I would never hear from her again. But about ten years later, I received two letters telling about her deliverance from demonic oppression. Laura is free today, but her deliverance came in a way that I did not expect. More of that later.

My purpose in telling this story is not to enter into the debate about whether Christians can be demon possessed. In the previous chapter, I already stated that a believer can never be owned by a demon because every Christian is "possessed" by God. We are indwelt by the Holy Spirit. Whatever disagreement there might be about this question, this is not the place to settle the matter.

·Nor do I tell this story to provide an example of how best to cast out evil spirits. Many counselors know much better than I what must be done when the Lauras of this world are harassed by evil personalities. Obviously, at least in this instance, my sincere attempts were unsuccessful.

My purpose in telling this story lies in another direction. First, I wish to show that even Christians can, at times, have the characteristics of Satan, for we still struggle in our fallenness. We can be bitter, rebellious, and malicious. In fact, there are more parallels than we care to admit.

Second, I wish to use Laura as an example of how the Serpent's poison can be neutralized. In other words, even though we sometimes act like the devil, we really don't have to. Laura reminds us that God has a higher purpose in these struggles. The moment we want to move beyond Christianity #101 we encounter resistance, but, in the end, we graduate to a new level of spiritual growth and development. This battle between us and Satan is a classroom in which we are taught to develop intimacy with God.

Satan wants us to sin so that we will be like him; God wants us to renounce evil and be filled with the Holy Spirit so that we will be like His Son. The more intense the temptation, the greater the triumph. As Christians, we have changed kingdoms and must now change our loyalties. But the battle within and without is intense.

THE STRUGGLES OF THE FLESH

Even if Satan were not free to roam the earth today, there would be murder, hatred, lying, moral impurity, and a litany of other sins. Take a look into your heart and you will see all the evils of the world in embryo. The devil does not have absolute power over human beings; he simply takes a bad situation and makes it worse. He tempts us with evil, but at the end of the day it is we who do what we want to do. Let us face up to our own sins, the sins of the flesh.

Now the deeds of the flesh are evident, which are: immorality, impurity, sensuality, idolatry, sorcery, enmities, strife, jealousy, outbursts of anger, disputes, dissensions, factions, envying, drunkenness, carousings, and things like these, of which I forewarn you, just as I have forewarned you, that those who practice such things shall not inherit the kingdom of God. (Galatians 5:19–21)

The seeds we plant can become deeply rooted in the soil of our mind and inflamed desires. What was thought to be a young sapling quickly becomes a sturdy tree.

Imagine that each branch of this tree is one of the "deeds of the flesh." Like the forbidden tree of Eden, each is appealing and each bears its own poisonous fruit. Though the branches appear to be separate, they are interrelated. We can trace them back to their roots.

These sins cover a wide range of behavior. Paul begins with moral impurity and ends with "carousings." But in between there is the occult practice of sorcery, strife, jealousy, drunkenness, and the like. There is something listed here that applies to all of us.

Second, and most important, all of these sins are hated by God. We might take comfort in the fact that we are not engaged in immorality, but do we have strife or outbursts of anger? Some of us might never be involved in sorcery or drunkenness, but do we have envy or enmities? These are all equally cursed. We must be careful not to judge others until we have judged ourselves. Our sins of the flesh are no more acceptable to God than those of someone else.

If the works of the flesh are the branches of this tree, what is its trunk? I believe the root is self-will, the desire to resist God's sovereignty in our lives. That was the sin of our first parents, and this rebellion has been passed on to us. Pride keeps me from letting God be the supreme ruler of my life.

Walt Whitman, in his epic poem "Song of Myself," said it all: "I have said that the soul is not more than the body, / And I have said that the body is not more than the soul, / And nothing, not God, is greater to one than one's self is."

Little wonder so many of us see ourselves as the center of God's three-ring circus. This "me-ism" lies at the heart of satanic rebellion. When Lucifer said "I will," his venom transformed him into an evil being. When Adam and Eve sinned, they were contaminated; now, as their children, we are all affected.

For Satan there is no cure; for us there is. We can, as it were, put the ax to the root of the tree. Rather than lopping off the same fruit from the same branches, we must, as best we can, ask God to give us the strength to make the tough choices that will affect the source of our sinful thoughts and behavior.

Our task is to identify the fruit of rebellion and give Satan no "place." If we are successful in our struggle against temptation,

God is glorified. To strike a blow to the flesh is to strike a blow to Satan. But first, we must see those character traits in us that remind us of the devil himself.

SOME CHARACTERISTICS OF THE SERPENT'S POISON

If we could see the devil himself in the midst of every sin, we would be more prudent, for while sin attracts us, the devil repels us. He is dangerous simply because he is invisible. He would not be as seductive if he were to suddenly appear. Though we abhor him, we often find ourselves comfortable with his attitudes and behaviors.

I have chosen these parallels between us and Satan because they remind us of how easily we can be like our archenemy. There are, I'm sure, other ways that we can be like him, but I have chosen these because of specific Scriptures that either directly teach or at least imply that we can, if we wish, still mirror our previous father of lies.

Verbal Slander

Even as the words left your mouth, you knew that you should not have said them. You spoke not so much in anger as in spite: You wanted to put that other person beneath you; you wanted your listener to make an implicit contrast between you and your opponent. Your words contained some truth, some exaggeration, but most of all the hidden desire to discredit him. Slander.

When Paul was giving the qualifications for the wives of deacons he wrote, "Women must likewise be dignified, not malicious gossips, but temperate, faithful in all things" (1 Timothy 3:11). In Greek, the expression "malicious gossips" is the one word *diabalous*, which, literally translated, means "devils." And the word *devil*, as we know, means "slanderer."

In saying that the wives of deacons should not be "devils," Paul is warning that they should control their tongues. They should not be found gossiping, giving a report about a person that is intended to harm. Even the truth, if told for the wrong reason and to the wrong person, is slander.

Gossip meets a deep perceived ego need within us. Gossip is the stirrup we use to hoist ourselves into the saddle. When we defame others, we are doing the devil's work for him. When we defame God's people, we promote the kingdom of darkness. We are acting with Satan's rationale and motivation. James wrote, "But no man can tame the tongue; it is a restless evil and full of deadly poison. With it we bless our Lord and Father; and with it we curse men, who have been made in the likeness of God" (James 3:8–9).

That "deadly poison" has its source in the Serpent. The one part of the body that Satan would most desire to control is our tongue. It has the power to bless and the power to curse; it has the ability to build the body of Christ and the power to tear it down. Paul's words apply to us all: *Don't be a devil!*

What difference is there between a believer who slanders the people of God and the Serpent who does the same? Both are sinning; both are doing what God hates; both are abetting the kingdom of darkness.

A Refusal to Confess Christ

Since self-will is the root of rebellion, it follows that Satan finds it difficult to confess to the lordship of Christ. "Therefore I make known to you that no one speaking by the Spirit of God says, 'Jesus is accursed'; and no one can say, 'Jesus is Lord,' except by the Holy Spirit (1 Corinthians 12:3). Satan will refrain from admitting that Christ is the Lord, except when forced to by God. No evil spirit would ever say this on his own.

I have met believers who cannot confess that Christ is Lord. They may be able to confess this in their hearts, but they cannot do it publicly. They find such submission to Christ nigh impossible, and speaking of Him as Lord is equally difficult for them. They cannot confess Christ even when God opens the door.

A Christian man told me that he was sitting in a barber's chair when the barber himself began asking questions about Christ and the Bible. The Christian told me, "I just found myself unable to speak. I had never witnessed before, and I didn't have a thing to say." Of course, sometimes such silence might be because of a lack of training. We all have had the fear that we would not be able to defend our views or answer questions others might ask. But often it is simply because we are ashamed that we belong to Christ; it is simply that we find it difficult to confess His lordship.

There is, I think, some similarity between a believer who

neglects to confess Christ as Lord and a demon who refuses to do so. Of course, the Christian desires to do so, whereas the demon does not. But the silent Christian and the rebellious demon have this in common: Both cannot find it within themselves to honor Christ in the presence of others.

We sing "O for a thousand tongues to sing," but our hesitancy to use the one we have might find its root in a lack of submission to the authority of Christ. God calls us to represent Him, not just by our lives, but by our lips. We can deny Christ not just by our stupidity, but also by our silence.

Uncleanness

At least twenty times in the New Testament demons are referred to as "unclean spirits." For example, the man from the country of the Gerasenes is described as having "an unclean spirit" (Mark 5:2). Obviously, this has nothing to do with physical cleanness, but rather with spiritual and moral impurity, that is, thoughts and actions that are shameful and degrading. To be unclean is to be out of moral agreement with God.

The same Greek word is used by Peter to refer to those teachers who indulge the flesh, teachers who have "corrupt desires" (2 Peter 2:10). This is the moral uncleanness that pollutes the conscience and defiles the mind. Turn on the television and you will see rampant uncleanness. Listen to the conversations in an office or factory and you will find uncleanness. Look at a newsstand and you will see uncleanness.

According to one survey, just over 50 percent of all Christian men confess to struggling with pornography in some form or other. It has been said, quite accurately, that each of us is like the moon: we have a dark side that no one sees. Only the Holy Spirit can shine the spotlight on that part of our lives. A woman confessed to burning three hundred trashy novels. She said it was like opening a desk drawer upside down and letting the junk spill out. An unclean mind was being cleansed.

Anything that is unlike God is impure. Once again, the similarity should not be overlooked. When we are self-driven rather than Spirit-driven, we will be unclean, and we will probably spend a great deal of mental energy trying to convince ourselves otherwise.

The Desire for Control

Demons want to control human beings, and, if necessary, they will even choose animals. When Christ expelled the demons from the man in the tombs, they requested that Christ send them into a herd of swine. Little wonder the animals ran into the river and drowned (Mark 5:11–13).

This desire for control is best seen in the false cults. Almost every one of these groups will cut you off from your family. They will tell you that you must break your friendship with those who hold opposing views. You are told that you now have a new family. Then the control begins. They will tell you how to dress, how to spend your money, and whom you can marry. They will tell you what to believe and how to live. And if you go "witnessing," it will not be alone; you will always have a senior member, just in case you will find someone who tries to get you to change your mind.

A man in the Chicago area began a cult, an offshoot of an evangelical church. One evening he had me over to discuss some matters and to tell me that he wanted me to come under his authority. He asked me to kneel at his coffee table and repent of my sins, specifically the sin of not being willing to submit to his leadership. I didn't do it for one good reason: I realized that he really did not want me to bow before God, but before him. He was, in effect, to be my god. Scary indeed.

We can see the extremes, but what about less-obvious desires for control? We've all met those who have to win every confrontation. They have to be the center of attention. They can never admit that they are wrong. They crave the power to dominate and manipulate. They manage their homes and offices by intimidation, subtle threats, and power plays. This control is so central to whom they perceive themselves to be that when they have to relinquish it, they become angry and lash out at those around them.

Another form of control is seen in those folks who jealously guard their resources and will not share them with others. They have a miserly spirit and desire to keep their grip on all that they have. They are poor souls, puzzled by the words of Christ, "It is more blessed to give than to receive" (Acts 20:35).

I know one Christian man who finally confessed his haughty, controlling spirit on his deathbed. Ultimately, he had to admit that there were some things that were slipping out of his hands.

Lying in a hospital room, with terminal cancer reducing him to helplessness, he finally had the humble spirit that should have characterized his lifetime.

A person who is deceived does not know it.

Control—the desire to own, possess, and command—is the fruit of self-will. It is just one more characteristic that we share, at least in some way, with the Evil One.

The Love of Praise

When Satan told Christ that He could have the kingdoms of this world in exchange for one act of worship, he revealed his deepest desire. Self-will craves recognition and adoration. It will protect, exalt, and draw attention to itself without any serious consideration of the price tag. The devil yearns for those moments when he is in the center, the object of exaggerated discussion and obedience.

Who of us has never been miffed because we were unrecognized, or because we were set aside in favor of someone who was less qualified? Reinforcing this desire for recognition is deceit, our carefully crafted ability to maintain an image of spirituality that is far removed from reality. When we are confronted by who we are inside, we lapse into denial, an unwillingness to face up to the truth of who we really are.

How easily we are offended; how easily are we angered if not recognized; how much are we like the devil, who exchanges the hotter fires of hell for a moment of worship.

Deceit

Satan is a deceiver and is also self-deceived. Certainly he was self-deceived when he fell in the ages past. How ironic that the one who said he would exalt himself to the greatest heights was brought down to the lowest depths. The gap between who he was and who he became must approach infinity. Deception indeed.

Deceit is tricky. Remember that a person who is deceived does not know it. If you knew that you were being deceived, the deception is not genuine. Please remember: *If you believe a lie, it becomes the truth for you.*

We are deceived about ourselves and overestimate our ability to rule our lives. We are deceived about God and think He makes unreasonable demands. We are deceived when we think that our way is best. We are deceived when we collapse into hopelessness and believe that God will not help us anymore.

Much of our deception is willful. We are often deceived because we long to be. Our ability to rationalize our behavior to appease our conscience must cause the good angels to marvel and the evil ones to rejoice. Our minds have the ability to rationalize whatever our hearts want to do. We can actually end up believing our own lies.

Just a week ago I heard the tragic story of a well-known and effective pastor who left his wife and went on an extended vacation with a woman in his congregation. He said that they had prayed about it and felt that this was "God's will." Can anyone doubt that indeed he had talked himself into believing that this actually was what God wanted? Can't you just see this man and his companion seeking God, yet wanting desperately to be deceived? Their wish evidently was granted.

Our ability to fool others and ourselves confirms the words of Jeremiah, "The heart is more deceitful than all else and is desperately sick; who can understand it?" (Jeremiah 17:9). Certainly we cannot understand our hearts; our capacity for deception is known but to God. Thus Jeremiah continues: "I, the Lord, search the heart, I test the mind, even to give to each man according to his ways, according to the results of his deeds" (v. 10).

If all of these characteristics are the fruit of self-will, then we must direct a series of blows to the trunk of the tree. We must ask God to give us the grace to "put to death" the deeds of the flesh, which mirror the deeds of our archenemy.

THE AX LAID TO THE ROOT OF THE TREE

Is there a cure for the self-will that has borne such bitter fruit? Ten years after my failed attempts at counseling Laura, she communicated with me. Here is the first of two letters:

A few years ago when I was experiencing demonic oppression, I had such a low self-image and was not able to experience the victory that had already been prepared for me through Jesus' blood. I was "beaten up" so to speak, with guilt, shame, despair, and hopelessness. I saw no way out.

After I left Chicago, I was involved in other churches where practically the same thing happened. I was not aware that I was being manipulated by demons to destroy the work of pastors and causing division among other Christians. I could not hold a job; therefore, for many years, I drifted in the same direction, namely, nowhere.

About a year ago I quit running. Besides, I had run out of places to run. With the Lord's help and the love and patience of the pastoral staff, plus the support and love of brothers and sisters in the body of Christ, I began to believe that God did love me and I could take Him at His Word. I determined to believe that I had victory in Christ and victory over the devil's evil schemes.

I realize now that I had believed lies. If we focus on what the enemy has planted in our minds, he has us defeated, just like he wants us. All the knowledge that I had obtained through the years was powerless because it was not coupled with faith. How could God love someone as awful as me? I thought, "He's going to leave you just as you are because he does not care." Those were the very words I listened to for years and believed them.

But praise be to God, He never gave up on me! I have come to accept my position in Christ. I am a joint-heir with Him and in a sense, enjoy His privileges. You can be sure that I keep short accounts with Him, and He has given me a tongue that gives Him praise and speaks confidently of all that I have been blessed with in Him.

Everything is not perfect; but I now enjoy a sense of freedom, a healthy self-esteem and victory, because "Whom the Son sets free, is free indeed." I desire to help others be freed from the bondage of the devil which is reinforced by his countless lies.

Thank you again for the part you played in recognizing that I was being tormented by evil spirits. Please continue to pray for me as I maintain a walk of victory.

May God bless you.

Sincerely in Christ,
Laura

The line that caught my attention was this: "All the knowledge I had obtained throughout the years was powerless because it was not coupled with faith"! Knowledge cannot help us unless we choose to believe it. But how can faith be built in our hearts? Of course, it comes through exposure to the Word of God, but along with it there must be a strong desire to turn our hearts and not just our heads toward God. Laura gave up the right to be angry and act like it, the right to be bitter and unforgiving, and the right to believe lies because they seemed more reasonable than the truth.

Dietrich Bonhoeffer, the German theologian who gave his life standing against Hitler, said, "When Christ calls a man He bids him come and die." To die to self-will does not mean that we are sad, gloomy, downcast, or introspective. It may or may not be a deeply emotional experience. True repentance often begins with remorse, but if it is biblical, it should end in joy.

Putting the ax to the root of the tree is not just one act, but a lifestyle. It is a daily acknowledgment of our dependence on Christ to have Him do what we cannot. Here are some truths to guide us.

1. *We must believe Christ has made our death to self-rule possible.* We read, "Knowing this, that our old self was crucified with Him in order that our body of sin might be done away with, that we should no longer be slaves to sin. . . . Therefore do not let sin reign in your mortal body that you should obey its lusts" (Romans 6:6, 12). To be "in Christ" is our position. But it is a real position, in which we have been declared righteous by God and therefore have permanent acceptance before our Father. This frees us from the discouragements we experience in trying to live the Christian life. We are loved by God; we have been elevated to a special position of honor. *Everything we are asked to do is based on what Christ has already done.*

The Cross not only was designed to take care of what I have done, but to make it possible to change who I am. The Cross was not merely to clean the impure water that comes from the fountain, but to fundamentally change the nature of the fountain itself. This is something God has done for me in Christ; it is also something that God continues to do. He knows we cannot crucify ourselves; crucifixion is something that someone else must do for us.

The New Testament has a healthy tension between the "already finished" and the "not yet" of our experience. Yes, in Christ we have died; yes, in Him we can be free; but it is not ours without a struggle, without the struggle of faith. Yet Christ died to make what appears to be impossible very possible. What you thought you could never do, God will give you the strength to accomplish.

Secure in these truths, we can give praise to God for our struggles. We must never lose sight of the truth repeated in this book, namely, that the devil exists for a purpose, and even our fleshly struggles are designed to strengthen us. God is well aware of how weak we are; He knows better than we how prone we are to return to our favorite sins. We must ever be done with the lie that our besetting sin is stronger than God's provision for us.

Remember, Satan wants us to ascribe to him what he does not have, namely, invincibility. He is as strong as we believe him to be. When Laura saw herself as helpless, she became as helpless as she thought she was. Only when she looked to the God of all hope, believing His promises to be true, was she led out of her discouragement.

In another letter to me, Laura said that the change in her attitude came when she began to give praise to God, rather than complaining to Him about her lot in life. She wrote, "Please tell others that a life of praise to the Lord is one of the most effective weapons against the enemy. Satan hates praises to Jesus and I have grown to love to use such praises against him."

2. *We must be repentant, that is, come to the end of our rationalizations and excuses.* Notice how weary Laura became. She says she had "no place to hide." God broke her. Because she was under new management, she was desperate enough to take orders from a different Master.

Why wasn't Laura helped earlier? Because she thought that her problem was greater than God's solution. She had an arsenal of excuses for behaving the way she did. Her defenses had long ago concluded that all of her problems were the fault of someone else. This is a common error we make when we believe our own emotions rather than the gracious promises of God. Satan's most strategic victory is to give us reasons to disbelieve what God has said.

Usually, God asks us to surrender the one thing that is most difficult—the one sin that we so jealously guard, rationalize, and cherish. If we say we cannot surrender it, we are denying that in

Christ we died to self-rule. We must submit to the Lord's rule in everything that our Father in heaven brings to our attention.

The devil says, "You can't."

God says, "You can."

3. *We must receive the filling of the Holy Spirit.* The works of the flesh stand in contrast to the fruit of the Spirit, which Paul says is "love, joy, peace, patience, kindness, goodness, faithfulness, gentleness, self-control" (Galatians 5:22–23). Paul promises, "Walk by the Spirit, and you will not carry out the desire of the flesh" (v. 16). Most of us think that if we put to death the desires of the flesh we will be rewarded with being able to walk in the Spirit. But Paul reverses the order for a good reason: He knows that we need the Spirit's power for even the very first steps of our walk. We must begin to walk in the Spirit even when we are weakest. We must learn to walk in the Spirit when we are in bondage, for only then will we be set free.

This power of the Spirit is received by faith. Each day we can claim the assurance that the Holy Spirit will be active in our lives. As we received Christ by faith, so we walk by faith. Only the Spirit can make us free and keep us that way.

4. *Finally, as already implied, the key is faith.* To quote from Laura's second letter, "I praise God that He cannot and will never lie. It was so hard through the years to believe in my victory because Satan made himself to appear very strong. He made me feel that I was no match for him and that he would never let me go. . . . Now I know better."

God is good. His promises are to be believed, and if we choose His way, God will do not only what is good for Him but also what is good for us. We must get beyond the notion that something has to be pleasant in order for it to be good. We must also get beyond the notion that if it is from Satan it is bad. Of course Satan *means* it to be bad, but God *means* it to be good. Satan's attacks can only be bad if we respond to them wrongly. Though he means harm, if we pass the test God will give us blessings. James wrote, "Blessed is a man who perseveres under trial; for once he has been approved, he will receive the crown of life, which the Lord has promised to those who love Him" (James 1:12). The trial is the trial of temptation.

When we are willing to put "to death the deeds of the body" (Romans 8:13), we will no longer tell God what He can and cannot use to refine us. The ownership of our lives will have been transferred, and we will believe that God is greater than our circumstances and the devil, who often is permitted to arrange them.

The vultures gather elsewhere when the carcasses have been removed.

The demons who have used our indwelling sins as a launching pad for their own harassment will find that their power is curtailed. They will find it more difficult to drive a wedge between us and God. They will find that the territory they once claimed has slipped from their grasp. They will be discouraged because we have repented of those things that have made us at least somewhat like them. The characteristics we share with the Serpent diminish, and we are transformed into the likeness of God's blessed Son. Christ-likeness becomes our first priority. Gazing on Christ, we become like Him.

Laura was eventually delivered from her demonic oppression without a confrontation with the spirits, without having them cast out. The sins the demons had so cleverly exploited disappeared under the blood of Christ. Faith grew in her heart, and the woman they had made so angry was singing praises to God. The woman who blamed others discovered that God helps only those who quit running and admit that the greatest need is the one that exists in their own hearts.

The vultures gather elsewhere when the carcasses have been removed from the premises. The flies that surround the rot leave when the dead vermin is buried. The wolf turns back when the sheep he has been pursuing stays close to the shepherd.

We have been bitten by a snake, but the wound has been lanced; there is a serum that neutralizes the effects of the venom. By faith, Christ came to set us "free indeed."

11

THE SERPENT IS
CAST OUT OF HEAVEN

God's judgment is often long in coming, but when it arrives it is swift and sure. When God begins to wrap up human history as we know it, the demise of the Serpent will happen in a series of stages. The lake of fire was inevitable from the moment Lucifer said, "I will make myself like the Most high" (Isaiah 14:14), but for centuries God has postponed the inevitable. When He no longer needs Satan for His own purposes, the end shall come.

At the Cross, the prince of this world was "cast out" (John 12:31). There Satan was judged and found to be guilty; his sentence of doom was held high for all to see. He was stripped of all authority and was shown to be deficient. As he writhed amid ashes of defeat and eventual doom, he was forced to concede that Christ was the victor. Satan took a blow to the head, whereas his retaliation was only a nip to Christ's heel. All things considered, Satan's was a pathetic show of strength.

Yes, lightning and thunder occur at the same time, but we see the lightning first and hear the roar of the thunder later. At the Cross, we saw the lightning; but there is a lapse of time before we hear the thunder. Satan continues to fight, no doubt communicating optimistic reports to his minions. But even now, as you read these pages, the war is over.

Satan's final ruin comes in three stages. First, he is cast out of heaven (the subject of this chapter). Second, he is bound for a thousand years. Finally, he is cast into the lake of fire (the subject of the next chapter). He knows as well as we do that these judgments are on the horizon. When he thinks of the future, he is terrified.

Does Satan have access to heaven today? The answer depends on how you understand Revelation 12. Some teach that Satan was cast out of heaven when Christ died on the cross. After all, Christ did say that "the ruler of this world will be cast out" (John 12:31). Also, Christ told His disciples that He saw "Satan like lightening fall from heaven." But it is unlikely that Christ was referring to Satan being cast out of heaven as described in Revelation 12. For one thing, Christ made this statement prior to the Cross, even before He predicted that the prince of this world would be cast out. For another, the disciples had just returned giving praise that demons had been cast out. Christ saw Satan fall through their ministry. The idea is that He "saw Satan *fallen*."

If Satan does have access to heaven today, as I believe he does, it is to continue his ongoing dialogue with God about us. Specifically, he comes to accuse, cajole, and receive permission to harass people on earth as God allows him. Though he is at war with all of humanity, his special attacks are aimed at those whom he knows will belong to God forever. Conceivably, dialogues such as those in the book of Job are happening today.

Other reasons I have for believing Satan has not yet been cast out of heaven will be given later. And, as we shall see, what we believe about the future has implications for how we conduct our warfare against Satan today.

Let us look at the details.

THE TWO GREAT SIGNS

"A great sign appeared in heaven: a woman clothed with the sun, and the moon under her feet, and on her head a crown of twelve stars; and she was with child; and she cried out, being in labor and in pain to give birth" (Revelation 12:1–2). This symbolism must be interpreted by other passages of Scripture. A careful look at this passage will indicate that it is not as difficult to understand it as it would appear.

This woman represents Israel; the twelve stars a symbol of the tribes; and the sun and moon remind us of Joseph's dream, where those heavenly bodies represented his parents, Jacob and Rachel. Further evidence that this is Israel is the fact that this woman will still be in existence during the Great Tribulation period.

The woman was about to give birth, a reference to Christ being born in Bethlehem. She gives birth to a son "who is to rule all the nations with a rod of iron; and her child was caught up to God and to His throne" (v. 5). This is a one-sentence summary of Christ's birth, life, and ascension into heaven.

The second sign is that of a "great red dragon having seven heads and ten horns, and on his heads were seven diadems" (v. 3). The crowns represent his authority; the ten horns evidently are the ten kingdoms described by Daniel 7:7–8, where we have a description of a unified Europe ruled under Satan's puppet, the Antichrist. Here the dragon who controls this political-religious system is red, perhaps a reminder that Satan is a murderer.

He was thrown out of heaven by one who . . . had been his underling!

There is more. "And his tail swept away a third of the stars of heaven and threw them to the earth" (v. 4). If these stars are angelic beings, as it seems likely, then this passage is a flashback to Satan's power to throw innumerable angels from heaven to the earth. We have already assumed that a third of the angels sided with him in his rebellion against God. John sees past and present events all brought together in a kaleidoscope. He sometimes will visualize events without identifying all the gaps in between.

The picture is intended to be grotesque. This evil dragon stands by waiting for the woman to give birth so that he can devour the child. We think immediately of Herod, who wanted to slay Christ when He was born in Bethlehem. This was the first in a series of attempts Satan made to kill the Christ.

The child escapes, of course. Mary, Joseph, and the Christ child flee into Egypt to thwart Herod's plans; and when they return to Nazareth, Christ is raised in their home like a normal child. Later he reveals Himself to be the Messiah, is rejected, and is crucified for the sin of the world. Then He is raised from the dead and taken up into heaven, just as this passage teaches.

Then John pictures this woman as fleeing into the wilderness, where she is protected and nourished for forty-two months, or three and one-half years. That refers to the last three and one-half years of the seven-year Tribulation period. Once again Satan wants to destroy the Jewish nation but fails in his attempt.

And now the best part.

THE WAR IN HEAVEN

We should not be surprised to find that Satan is still in heaven. Evidently God has continued to grant him some of the same privileges that he had before his rebellion. But now, he is about to leave the glories of heaven, never to return. He must catch a last glimpse of the glory, for he shall not enter those courts again. What an eternity of memories he shall carry with him!

Though Michael had so much respect for Satan that he would not contend with him over the body of Moses (Jude 9), he now fights with unerring confidence. "And there was war in heaven, Michael and his angels waging war with the dragon. . . . And they were not strong enough, and there was no longer a place found for them in heaven" (Revelation 12:7–8). Let us not forget that at one time Michael and Lucifer were colleagues; they served the same master and had essentially the same responsibilities. Since it is likely that Michael had at one time served under Lucifer, the loss of this battle was especially painful for the devil. *He was thrown out of heaven by one who at one time had been his underling!*

This is the heavenly counterpart to Christ's victory on earth. The victory of the Cross was now translated into a victory in heaven. The devil and his angels are thrown out and "lose their place in heaven." The Serpent glances toward heaven for the last time and knows that for him the gates are now bolted shut.

Imagine his anger when he sees the gates of heaven close with the saints he had persecuted on earth now standing before the throne of God in the spotless beauty of Jesus! He sees them exalted above the angels, as brothers of Christ, though they had committed many of the same sins as he. He knows that they will be there forever; he also knows where *he* will be forever. No wonder he is furious.

A further reason for saying that this event happens in the middle of the Tribulation period is that the coming kingdom is announced as about to begin. "Then I heard a loud voice in heaven, saying, 'Now the salvation, and the power, and the kingdom of our God and the authority of His Christ have come, for the accuser of our brethren has been thrown down, he who accuses them before our God day and night'" (v. 10). This kingdom could only be proclaimed because Satan, the accuser of the brethren, had been cast down. If we interpret this kingdom to be the millennial kingdom, that is, the coming literal reign of Christ on earth, then it appears that Satan is thrown out of heaven to prepare for this special rule of Christ.

Also, the interval between the war in heaven and Satan's imprisonment during the millennial reign appears to be a short period of time. After he is cast out, we read, "Woe to the earth and the sea, because the devil has come down to you, having great wrath, knowing that he has only a short time" (v. 12). He hits the earth running, for he is very angry.

If Satan was cast out of heaven when Christ died, this "short time" would have turned out to be some two thousand years so far. It is more likely that John wants us to understand that the devil is angry because he has only three and one-half years left before Christ returns in glory and Satan is confined in the abyss during the millennial period.

A final reason it makes good sense to think of this as an end-time scenario is that Satan continues his persecution of Israel, a persecution that takes place during the Tribulation period. We read, "And when the dragon saw that he was thrown down to the earth, he persecuted the woman who gave birth to the male child" (v. 13). The woman now flees into the wilderness, where she is nourished for "a time and times and half a time." This refers to a period of three and one-half years; "a time" is one year, "times" is two years, and "half a time" is six months (cf. Daniel 7:25; 12:7; Revelation 11:2; 13:5). Thus this final persecution lasts three and one-half years.

He who has always desired to destroy the promised seed so that the purposes and plans of God might not be fulfilled now makes one last attempt to exterminate the nation of Israel. Pursuing the woman, the Serpent originates a flood to sweep the woman away, but the earth swallowed up the water. Whatever this might mean, it is clear that it is one last satanic effort to destroy the nation. In some way, God assists the Israelites so that they are not completely wiped out.

SATAN'S SHINING MOMENT

And suddenly it appears as if Satan's goal is within reach! Losing his place in heaven made him only more determined to succeed on earth. During the last three and one-half years of the Tribulation period, Satan, through Antichrist, rules the world. Though he knows his time is short, he wants to make the best of it. We read these stunning words:

> And it was given to him to make war with the saints and to overcome them, and authority over every tribe and people and tongue and nation was given to him. All who dwell on the earth will worship him, everyone whose name has not been written from the foundation of the world in the book of life of the Lamb who has been slain. (Revelation 13:7–8)

By the time Antichrist appears, the world will be ready to deify a leader if he appears to have what it takes to unite the world and bring in an era of peace. It is not enough for Satan to inhabit a man who will claim to be God. The master deceiver will actually try to duplicate the three members of the Trinity. These three personalities will do their best to try to confuse the world by pretending to be the true and living God.

First, Satan himself corresponds to God the Father, and he is spoken of as the "dragon" who gives his authority to the beast who is Antichrist (13:4). Thus Satan does want the world to think he is God. This dream will shortly become a nightmare.

Second, there is the beast who is empowered by the dragon, who corresponds to Christ. He will try his best to do miracles and duplicate Christ's resurrection. Specifically, we read, "I saw one of his heads as if it had been slain, and his fatal wound was healed. And the whole earth was amazed and followed after the beast" (13:3). The world will believe that the Antichrist survived a wound that would have put any other man to death. The skeptical will be convinced that this is the man to follow and worship.

At last there will be religious unity. The dragon and the beast will receive the worship of the world. Yes, all who dwell upon the earth will worship him, except the elect whose names were written in the Book of Life from before the foundation of the world. Apart from the relatively few who have the courage to oppose this dictator, he will capture the hearts of the world.

During the apex of Hitler's career, the Lord's Prayer was changed by many to read, "Our Father Adolf who art in Nuremberg, the Third Reich come." In the same way people will worship Antichrist, who has had the financial wizardry to put the world on a stable economic base. He will be the one who is deemed worthy of the praise accorded him.

The third member of this unholy Trinity is referred to as the second beast in Revelation 13:11–18. Just as the Holy Spirit draws attention to Christ, so the assignment of this evil man is to get the world to worship Antichrist. "And he makes the earth and those who dwell in it to worship the first beast, whose fatal wound was healed" (v. 12). To gain the confidence of the world, this beast performs great miracles. Many of the wonders performed by this unholy triad are specified: Fire will come down from heaven, images will be caused to speak (possibly this will be accomplished through trickery, since it is unlikely that Satan can create life), and the fatal wound will be healed.

How will Antichrist gain such awesome religious power? He will do some things that people think only God can do. Paul writes of him that he will be "in accord with the activity of Satan, with all power and signs and false wonders, and with all the deception of wickedness for those who perish, because they did not receive the love of the truth so as to be saved" (2 Thessalonians 2:9–10). The three words used here—*power, signs,* and *wonders*—are all used of the miracles of Christ. Antichrist's power to duplicate the works of Christ is so remarkable that multitudes will believe.

Hitler said that a big lie is always more effective than a small one. If so, the lie that man is God will be very effective. A nation schooled in what is known today as New Age thought will believe. This is Satan's contorted attempt at keeping his promise to Eve, "You will be like God."

Satan's fondest wish will be realized. The whole world is worshiping his man, but standing behind him is Satan. In actuality, the whole world is worshiping him!

AT LAST, CONTROL!

According to a Barna research report, about two-thirds of Americans believe that the different religions of the world are actually worshipers of the same God. This vision of religious unity is what will propel the world to one-world religion and one-world government. Religion and politics will come together in one person; the science of mind and the science of economics will blend into unified world philosophy.

Today there is a network of organizations committed to bringing about a unified world order to address the problems of war, hunger, and economic instability. Leading the pack will be a world ruler who has the charisma to unify the religions of the world and weld a political structure that has the muscle to forge a global organization. He will be both priest and king, messiah and emperor.

This ruler will gain his strength from the same source as Adolf Hitler, who controlled Germany with such hypnotic magnetism that the people found him practically irresistible. Hitler was taken through deep levels of occult transformation so that, in the words of one of his friends, "his body was but the shell for the spirit that inhabited him."

All of the original doctrines found in the third chapter of Genesis will surface: the deity of mankind, the transformation of consciousness ("enlightenment"), moral relativism, and the like. Possibly even reincarnation might be used to spread the word that some great historical personage of the past has reappeared. Think of the awe and worship that would come to the person who could claim to have been "raised from the dead" by being recycled into our mode of existence.

He will usher in a religion that will counterfeit Christianity at every point. Instead of prayers, there will be mantras; instead of preachers, there will be gurus; in the place of prophets, there will be psychics; in the place of the Ten Commandments, there will be new commandments for this new age.

Now that Satan's puppet is in place, he will be able to control the world through a vast financial network based on stringent controls. No one will be able to buy or sell without the "mark of the beast." Those who challenge his authority will be put to death. Also like Hitler, the new messiah will hate the Jews with a vengeance.

Predictions about such a world system have been made for years in New Age literature. H. G. Wells said that someday there would be a worldwide revolution consisting of a great multitude and variety of overlapping groups "all organized for collective and political and social educational as well as propagandist action."[1] He continues:

> It will be a great world movement as widespread and evident as socialism or communism. It will largely take the place of these movements. It will be more. It will be a world religion. The large loose assimilatory mass of the groups and societies will be definitely and obviously attempting to swallow up the entire population of the world and become the new human community.[2]

This, then, is the culmination to which all the various strands of religious unity are headed. Even the tributaries of satanic worship that we see today might be the very ones that will flow into a single river of occult religion. Here is the apex of the godhood of man. At last, the problems of the world will be overcome—and with spiritual solutions.

Under the guise of laudable slogans, the deification of man will reach its most striking affirmation. All opposition will be set aside, and the New World Order will be in place.

For those who do not get on board, there will be intimidation, starvation, and liquidation.

The devil will be in charge.

THE OVERCOMERS

Whatever scenario we might adopt regarding the end times, it is clear that there are believers during the Tribulation period when Satan through Antichrist rules the world. Some would point to the existence of these believers as proof that the church will go through the Tribulation period. They will be protected from the direct wrath of God but suffer persecution and death at the hands of the dragon.

My preference is to believe that while the church will be raptured before the Tribulation begins, there will be a remnant (primarily Jews) who will be saved during the Tribulation period. Whichever scenario is adopted, all are agreed that godly people will be challenged to overcome the beast.

And how does this believing remnant counteract the attack of Satan? Just as we do. "And they overcame him because of the blood of the Lamb and because of the word of their testimony, and they did not love their life, even when faced with death" (Revelation 12:11).

First, they overcame him by the blood of the Lamb. Satan can no longer accuse those who have been acquitted by God, thanks to the sacrifice of Christ. Every just accusation is now silenced. As we read, "To Him who loves us and released us from our sins by His blood" (Revelation 1:5). No matter how extensive Satan's end-time network, the power of the Cross still stands. Indeed, the power of the Cross is seen most clearly when the forces of evil seem to triumph.

The proclaimation of the gospel ... enables us to stand against the rage of Satan.

Even those of us who have been schooled in the Christian faith often do not grasp the significance of the blood of Christ, the basis for our forgiveness and victory. At the end of a difficult day of failure and sin, we are tempted to come to God, telling Him that we really don't expect to have our prayers answered because we have failed so miserably. In contrast, when we have had a good day, and our relationship with God appears to be on target, we think that surely God will hear us.

In both instances we err. Whether our day has been good or bad, our basis for approaching God is always the same, namely, the blood of Christ. And whether our guilt is objective (the guilt that appears before God) or subjective (the feelings of guilt we have within our own consciences), the remedy is always the same: the blood of Christ.

When Moses was in Egypt, the homes of the Israelites were spared because of the blood on their doors. It mattered not whether the families inside had a good day or a bad day; it mattered not whether they had been successful in overcoming sin, important though that was. What mattered was the blood. For God said, "When I see the blood I will pass over you" (Exodus 12:13).

Second, they overcame him by the "word of their testimony" (Revelation 12:11). The proclamation of the gospel, the assertion that Christ died for us and we have experienced His victory—this is what enables us to stand against the rage of Satan. This, after all, is the only hope for our country and our culture.

Third, the gift of martyrdom is also what kept Satan from winning a victory. John wrote: "And they did not love their life even to death" (v. 11). These believers will die under the rule of a revived Roman Empire, just as the early Christians died under the rule of the old Roman Empire. In both cases, their martyrdom is what God has willed. Satanic forces might instigate the *destroying;* but God does the *delegating.* Just as it was God's will for Christ to die at the hands of evil men, so His followers die under the same care and providential plan. Even here, the devil is still God's servant.

As Luther wrote,

> Let goods and kindred go,
> This mortal life also;
> The body they may kill:
> God's truth abideth still,
> His Kingdom is forever.

Death cannot frighten those who follow the Prince of Life.

But the heady days of the Serpent are short-lived. God will not allow this counterfeit leadership to go uncontested for one good reason: The Father will not for long tolerate a man who takes the worship that belongs to His Son. The giddy optimism about man's ability to rule the world is about to end. Satan's day is about over.

The showdown is just days away.

12

THE SERPENT IN
ETERNAL HUMILIATION

W e can only speculate what might have happened if Lucifer had been shown the lake of fire before he made his decision to rebel. If only he had believed that God always knows best, his tragic story might have read differently. But now, centuries of sadistic rebellion will never compensate for one hour in the lake of fire. And the fire will never be quenched.

In the Old Testament, God repeatedly predicted a coming kingdom in which righteousness and justice would prevail. He spoke of a day when men will lay down their weapons and live together in tranquillity and peace. "And they will hammer their swords into plowshares and their spears into pruning hooks. Nation will not lift up sword against nation, and never again will they learn war" (Isaiah 2:4). Needless to say, such political tranquillity has never happened in recorded history. This will be a kingdom in which Christ will rule.

Repeatedly, Satan has attempted to usher in this kingdom under his own auspices. The Roman Empire, with its vast network of cruel armies, roads, and laws, was the first clear attempt to unify the world and bring it under a central leadership. However, Satan discovered that he cannot control human beings at will; he cannot establish a kingdom on earth that is both organized and unified. This empire eventually disintegrated into brutality and factions. The selfishness of man makes all attempts at teamwork futile.

Building on the ruins of the fall of Rome came the so-called Holy Roman Empire, an unholy union between the political and religious powers of Europe. With the coming of Napoleon, this empire, which had long since fragmented, was pronounced nonexistent. Again, though many of Satan's dreams for a political system in league with counterfeit religion were realized, in the end, that too came unraveled. This was the end of what became known as the *First Reich* (Rule).

Then the German state of Prussia arose in power, and under the leadership of Bismarck, picked up the ruins left after the Napoleonic wars. A new empire with a new Caesar (Kaiser) was established with the express intention of unifying Europe and fulfilling the dream of a revived empire. But this second grand attempt failed when Germany lost World War I. Thus ended the *Second Reich*.

Satan will make one more massive attempt to rule the world.

When a young soldier was told that Germany had been defeated in November of 1918, he wept for the first time since his mother died. It was then that he had a mystical experience of being one with the universe; he records that at that moment he felt his call into politics. He had witnessed the end of the Second Reich, but out of its ruins he dreamed about making another grand attempt.

And so it was that Hitler inaugurated his *Third Reich*, the third attempt to unify the world under a single leader. He boasted that his Reich would last for one thousand years. But, as we now know, it was in existence for only some twelve years and six months. So much for Satan's ability to incite the nations toward unity and world domination!

The world has never been unified, much less has one ruler

ever been able to sit on a worldwide seat of power. The thought of world unity is tantalizing, given the problems of hunger and war. To bring about an effective and stable economy, the world, we are told, should be anxious to come together in one family of nations.

We have learned that the Bible teaches that Satan will make one more massive attempt to rule the world—and will finally succeed. By the time Antichrist appears, the world will be ready to attempt a dream that has been in the making since the days of Babylon when all the people chose to stay together, unified by a tower whose top would "reach into heaven" (Genesis 11:4). Given today's advance in technology and instant communication, a unified world will appear to be possible.

Satan will be thrown out of heaven in the middle of the Tribulation period. But this will not hinder him from establishing his global network. Indeed, it is his fury, knowing that his time is short, that will motivate him to take one last, daring gamble. He will rival Christ by ruling the world. This will be the *Fourth Reich.*

All will not be well within his empire. For one thing, the saints of God will oppose him. For another, the rulers of the world will move to protect their own selfish interests. The fragile unity of the world will begin to crumble. And, most important, the hatred toward the Jews will be so rampant that the Middle East will be turned into a volatile military powder keg. And that will prove to be his undoing.

This conflict, known as the Battle of Armageddon, will be the worst in the history of the world. Though it might begin in the valley of Megiddo, it soon spills throughout the whole land of Israel and the Middle East. Christ said of those days, "For then there will be great tribulation, such as has not occurred since the beginning of the world until now, nor ever will be" (Matthew 24:21). The total depravity of the human race will again be proven.

This time the conflict between Christ and the devil will not take place in the Judean hills, but on the Mount of Olives. Satan will not confront a Christ who is weakened by hunger, but a glorified Christ who comes suited for war. The rightful ruler is on His way, and Satan knows it.

THE GLORIOUS RETURN OF CHRIST

The armies of the earth will then gather in Israel in battle over the city of Jerusalem. Then Christ shall return. Zechariah wrote:

> For I will gather all the nations against Jerusalem to battle, and the city will be captured, the houses plundered, the women ravished, and half the city exiled, but the rest of the people will not be cut off from the city. Then the Lord will go forth and fight against those nations, as when He fights on a day of battle. In that day His feet will stand on the Mount of Olives, which is in front of Jerusalem on the east; and the Mount of Olives will be split in its middle from east to west by a very large valley, so that half of the mountain will move toward the north and the other half toward the south. (Zechariah 14:2–4)

Geologists tell us that there is a fault line on the Mount of Olives that winds all the way to the Dead Sea. When the feet of Christ step upon the mount, it will divide from east to west. The warring nations will then stop fighting each other and turn on Christ. Now Satan will have one final opportunity to topple Christ from His throne and throw His crown to the ground. But as Satan has had to discover repeatedly, the conflict will be only a charade.

John describes it this way:

> And I saw heaven opened, and behold, a white horse, and He who sat upon it is called Faithful and True, and in righteousness He judges and wages war. His eyes are a flame of fire, and on His head are many diadems; and He has a name written upon Him which no one knows except Himself. He is clothed with a robe dipped in blood, and His name is called The Word of God. And the armies which are in heaven, clothed in fine linen, white and clean, were following Him on white horses. From His mouth comes a sharp sword, so that with it He may smite the nations, and He will rule them with a rod of iron; and He treads the wine press of the fierce wrath of God, the Almighty. And on His robe and on His thigh He has a name written, "KING OF KINGS, AND LORD OF LORDS."
>
> Then I saw an angel standing in the sun, and he cried out with a loud voice, saying to all the birds which fly in midheaven, "Come, assemble for the great supper of God; so that you may eat the flesh of kings and the flesh of commanders and the flesh of mighty men and the flesh of horses and of those who sit on them and the flesh of all

men, both free men and slaves, and small and great."

And I saw the beast and the kings of the earth and their armies, assembled to make war against Him who sat on the horse and against His army. And the beast was seized, and with him the false prophet who performed the signs in his presence, by which he deceived those who had received the mark of the beast and those who worshiped his image; these two were thrown alive into the lake of fire which burns with brimstone. And the rest were killed with the sword which came from the mouth of Him who sat upon the horse, and all the birds were filled with their flesh. (Revelation 19:11–21)

Who are those who accompany Him, "clothed in fine linen, white and clean" (v. 14)? They are not angels, but the saints who have just eaten at the marriage supper of the Lamb (vv. 7–9). Since there is evidence that the believers who are presently on earth will already have been raptured before these incredible events, these saints include the present believers in this age.

Catch your breath as you read this: *We will follow Christ to subdue the nations of the earth in the final battle of history!* We will stand with Him on the Mount of Olives and march with Him to victory. Those who have never had the good fortune to visit the land of Israel in this life will get the grand tour in the next. Christ Himself shall lead His people into victory.

As for the beast and the false prophet, they are "thrown alive into the lake of fire which burns with brimstone" (v. 20). Satan will share their fate with them, but not just yet. He still has one intermediate stop before he joins those whom he so cruelly deceived and controlled. The kingdom age is about to dawn, and God still needs him to fulfill a final purpose. The fact that he is spared the lake of fire for now does not make his future there any less certain. History now marches with inevitable certainty.

THE SERPENT IN THE KINGDOM

When Christ confronted the demon-possessed man who lived among the tombs, the demons begged that they might not be cast into the abyss; they feared being tormented before their time (Matthew 8:29; Luke 8:31). Christ granted their request and allowed them to enter a herd of swine, which then promptly ran into a lake and was drowned.

But the demons were able only to postpone—not cancel—

their doom. Now that the kingdom is established under its rightful king, Satan and those who are his are for a time confined to the abyss which they so much feared. We read:

> *Then I saw an angel coming down from heaven, holding the key of the abyss and a great chain in his hand. And he laid hold of the dragon, the Serpent of old, who is the devil and Satan, and bound him for a thousand years; and threw him into the abyss, and shut it and sealed it over him, so that he should not deceive the nations any longer, until the thousand years were completed; after these things he must be released for a short time.* (Revelation 20:1–3)

Why are Satan and his demons bound? One more time, God will demonstrate the bankruptcy of human nature. Though Satan is not allowed to deceive the nations during Christ's reign, the nations are still led astray by the inherent wickedness of human nature. So after Satan is loosed at the end of the one thousand years, he finds those who are willing to side with him in one final assault on God. "When the thousand years are completed, Satan will be released from his prison, and will come out to deceive the nations which are in the four corners of the earth, Gog and Magog, to gather them together for the war; the number of them is like the sand of the seashore" (20:7–8). No one knows who these nations are; what seems clear is that they are not the Gog and Magog referred to in Ezekiel 38. This is a different time and a different place.

What we do know is that these nations now gather round Jerusalem in a gasping, vain attempt to dethrone Christ. "And they came up on the broad plain of the earth and surrounded the camp of the saints and the beloved city, and fire came down from heaven and devoured them" (Revelation 20:9). This, then, is the last flicker of hope for Satan; if he thinks he can still win against God, it is only because he has now come to believe his own lies. It is the last direct conflict in which he will participate. The lake of fire is but a step away.

The prophetic scheme I have outlined is known as *premillennialism,* the belief that Christ will yet rule over this earth with His capital in Jerusalem. This view takes the prophecies of the Old Testament more literally than other interpretations of the kingdom.

To be fair, I must mention that many believe that we will

bring in the kingdom on earth; then Christ will return to crown our efforts. Even Christians who should have known better have taught what theologians call *postmillennialism*, that is, the idea that we will usher in the kingdom and then Christ will return to wrap up history. This optimistic view of our efforts has been discredited, but still has some adherents in our time. Thankfully, their numbers are few.

There are many more who believe that we are already in the kingdom age. Christ's coming will not lead to the establishment of the kingdom because the kingdom is the church, they say. This view is known as *amillennialism*, that is, the belief that there is no coming kingdom. All the kingdom promises to Israel are either conditional, or they are being fulfilled to the church. This teaching has had able adherents throughout the history of the church.

Obviously this is not the place to try to resolve these disputes. But these differing views have practical implications: If the church is the kingdom, this means that Satan is *already* bound in this age. His activity would not just be limited, but nonexistent on the earth. To be bound in the abyss means that he is not free to roam the earth.

Jay Adams, whose books on counseling have been helpful to many, believes that even now we are in the kingdom age and Satan is bound. This curtailment, or restraint, he says, "involved the virtual cessation of such activity [demonic possession] by his demonic forces. This accounts for the rare incidence, if not the entire absence of demonic possession in modern times."[1]

I strongly disagree with this view, of course. There are, in my judgment, powerful biblical reasons to believe that this is not the age of the kingdom. Much less should we assume that there is little or no demon possession today. If this were the kingdom age, his activity would not just be "curtailed" but would have come to a complete halt. If this were the kingdom age, we would have no contact with the roaring lion who goes about "seeking someone to devour" (1 Peter 5:8). The New Testament teaching regarding our conflict with the devil could be conveniently brushed aside.

The evidence that Christ will yet rule this earth from Jerusalem is convincing. Surely David understood Nathan's prediction to mean that he would bear a son who would someday rule over his kingdom, that is, the kingdom over which David himself ruled (2 Samuel 7:8–17). And the angel Gabriel told Mary that her child would be great and the "Lord God will give Him the throne of His father David; and He will reign over the house of Jacob forever; and His kingdom will have no end" (Luke 1:32). It is doubtful that Mary or any of her contemporaries would have believed that this kingdom was in heaven. David's kingdom was on this earth with its capital in Jerusalem.

But there is a related reason why I believe Christ will rule from this earth: He must prove that He can do what Satan could not. This contaminated earth, which has been the chief sphere of Satan's activities for millennia, must be the very place where Christ Himself yet rules in glory and triumph. *Christ who delivered the knockout punch will rule on Satan's turf.*

If the devil is God's devil, then hell is God's hell.

If the first step in Satan's demise is that he is forbidden to reside in heaven, then the second step is that he is forbidden to reside on earth. For one thousand years the nations are permitted to go their own way without satanic direction or influence.

Satan's remorse is now magnified. Milton captured this despairing sense of permanent isolation from God. "Which way I fly is Hell; myself am Hell." He who had always taken his own hell with him, now is about to be cast into a hell of a different sort. He must now relinquish control of all beings he ever influenced. The power is gone, so also is the insolence, scheming, and defiance. Stripped of everything he once thought he had, he is now forced to abide in eternal darkness.

THE LAKE OF FIRE

We are now ready for the final stage in Satan's demise.

"And the devil who deceived them was thrown into the lake of fire and brimstone, where the beast and the false prophet are also; and they will be tormented day and night forever and ever" (Revelation 20:10). At last he joins his cohorts in eternal torment. No doubt he will discover that it is even worse than he imagined.

What can we say about the eternal state of Satan in the lake of fire?

1. *This place was created by God, prepared by the Almighty for the inhabitants who were doomed to indwell it.* Christ said that God will say to the wicked, "Depart from Me, accursed ones, into the eternal fire which has been prepared for the devil and his angels" (Matthew 25:41).

God has prepared two eternal destinies. "I go to prepare a place for you," Christ told His disciples (John 14:2). That place, heaven, is even now ready to receive those who will be with God forever. As for the lake of fire, it also has been prepared. Though no one is yet in hell today (the unbelieving dead go to hades), Christ implies that the lake of fire has nevertheless already been prepared. Though now empty, it is being readied in anticipation of its occupants.

Let us say boldly that the lake of fire is not simply a spin-off of the natural creation, but is actually a specific place created for a specific reason. And the Creator rules whatever He creates. Not even here does God abandon His sovereign rule. If the devil is God's devil, then hell is God's hell.

God, not the devil, rules in hell. He is the Creator, and He does not give a part of His kingdom to another. Hell is neither the figment of a lively imagination, nor is it the place where Satan will have his kingdom. God is in the heavens above and, because He is omnipresent, He is in hell below. Even there, properly interpreted, His will is done.

Consider: Hell is a place of judgment for the rebellion of God's creatures. But, as we shall see, these judgments are meticulously meted out, all under the watchful supervision of God. The penalties must be just, accurate, and commensurate with the offense. God would never delegate the delicate task of justice to another.

2. *Hell is a place of torment.* The impression, often given in medieval folklore, is that hell is the devil's domain; we get the idea that here he rules, giving orders to his own demons and harassing people at will. Dante, we learned, painted a picture of

hell with the demons tormenting those who arrive at this destination. His pitchfork was thought to be a kind of medieval billy club used to inflict torture. This, of course, is based on mythology, not the Bible.

We must look at the text carefully. We read: "They will be tormented day and night forever and ever" (Revelation 20:10). This is not where Satan torments others, but where he is tormented. He is not the torment*or*, but the torment*ed*. He is scarcely in a position to trouble others, for he himself is overcome by the troubles heaped upon him.

The Serpent's state in hell is even more pitiful than that of other creatures! Those who have sinned greatly are punished greatly. No one sinned with more knowledge and more light than Lucifer. His judgment will be in line with his rebellion. Be assured there is no *king* in hell!

J. Marcellus Kik suggests, perhaps quite rightly,

> What a welcome will the Devil receive from those whom he has deceived! What curses, what vituperations, what abuses, what reviling, what berating will be heaped upon his head! He will be surrounded by a lake of curses. His nostrils cannot escape the stench of vituperation. It is part of his torment day and night. He will be hated, despised and rejected for all of eternity.[2]

Yes, it is quite true that Satan will never sing again. He will only howl. The memory of heaven's choirs will only magnify the torment of his own regret. And there is no exit.

3. *Hell has many occupants.* When the devil is thrown into hell, we read that this is where "the beast and the false prophet are also" (Revelation 20:10). They have been there since the return of Christ which, by this time, will have happened a thousand years before. We have already read of their fate. "And the beast was seized, and with him the false prophet who performed the signs in his presence, by which he deceived those who had received the mark of the beast and those who worshiped his image; these two were thrown alive into the lake of fire which burns with brimstone" (Revelation 19:20). So far as we know, they are hell's first occupants. No doubt the other fallen angels enter along with their master, Apollyon.

But hell also has human occupants. Those who are not sheltered from the wrath of God by Christ must bear their own fate.

Immediately after the devil's arrival into the lake of fire, we read of the judgment of all unbelieving dead. They are judged according to their works.

> *Then I saw a great white throne and Him who sat upon it, from whose presence earth and heaven fled away, and no place was found for them. And I saw the dead, the great and the small, standing before the throne, and books were opened; and another book was opened, which is the book of life; and the dead were judged from the things which were written in the books, according to their deeds. And the sea gave up the dead which were in it, and death and Hades gave up the dead which were in them; and they were judged, every one of them according to their deeds. Then death and Hades were thrown into the lake of fire. This is the second death, the lake of fire. And if anyone's name was not found written in the book of life, he was thrown into the lake of fire.* (Revelation 20:11–15)

Hades, the place where the unbelieving dead now reside, will then be cast into the lake of fire. Along with Satan and his demons will be millions of others who will be judged on the basis of what they did with what they knew. Their suffering can never pay for their sins, so it must go on eternally.

4. *Hell is eternal.* Though there are many who insist that hell is a place of annihilation, this simply does not do justice to the texts of Scripture. We are told that they are "tormented day and night forever and ever" (20:10). Unceasing restlessness; unceasing hopelessness; unceasing regret.

Some scholars take the words of Christ in Matthew 10:28— "Rather fear Him who is able to destroy both soul and body in hell"—to mean that souls are destroyed (annihilated) by the flames of hell. But the word *destroyed* does not mean annihilation; there is an eternal destruction, a conscious torment that never ends. The souls in hell will not be destroyed in the sense that they are annihilated; they will be destroyed in the sense that they will be tormented without the hope of future recovery or fulfillment.

Christ taught that hell was as eternal as heaven. "These will go away into eternal punishment, but the righteous into eternal life" (Matthew 25:46). If we believe that we will enjoy eternal life forever, we must believe that others will suffer eternal punishment forever. Unfortunately, we are not free to choose our beliefs based on our preferences.

5. *Hell is just.* To us as humans, everlasting punishment is disproportionate to the offense committed. God appears to be cruel, unjust, sadistic, and vindictive. The purpose of punishment, we are told, is always redemptive. Rehabilitation is the goal of all prison sentences. The concept of a place where there will be everlasting punishment without any possibility of parole or reform seems unjust.

But we must remember that all beings, whether demonic or angelic, will be judged on the basis of knowledge. More will be required from those who have been given much. The Serpent, needless to say, cannot plead ignorance. His decision was made with a knowledge of the facts before him. Of course he didn't know everything, since such full knowledge belongs only to God, but he knew enough to be severely judged for his stupidity.

God judges with a full knowledge of all the facts. No motive will be misinterpreted; no extenuating circumstances will be overlooked. Unlike a human court, which can shelve details or misinterpret them, God's knowledge extends both to that which has happened in the world and to that which might have happened under different circumstances.

Satan and those who will join him in the lake of fire are eternally guilty. No suffering of the creature can ever repay the Creator. If suffering could erase even the most insignificant sin, then those in hell would eventually be freed after their debt was paid. But all creaturely suffering could not so much as cancel a single sin.

Sir Francis Newport, who ridiculed Christianity, is quoted as saying these terrifying words on his deathbed:

> Oh, that I was to lie a thousand years upon the fire that never is quenched, to purchase the favor of God, and be united to him again! But it is a fruitless wish. Millions and millions of years would bring me no nearer to the end of my torments than one poor hour. Oh, eternity, eternity! forever and ever! Oh, the insufferable pains of hell![3]

6. *We cannot comprehend the seriousness of sin.* We must confess that we do not know how much punishment is enough for Satan, who bears the greater responsibility, or for man, who bears the lesser. The famous Jonathan Edwards said that the reason we find hell to be so offensive is because of our insensitivity to sin.

What if, from God's standpoint, the greatness of the sin is determined by the honor of the One against whom it is committed? Then the guilt of sin is infinite because it is the violation of the character of an infinite Being. And thus, God would deem that such infinite sins deserve an infinite penalty.

As humans we can be thankful that we do not have to bear our sin. An infinite Being came to pay an infinite price so that we could be redeemed. "To Him who loves us and released us from our sins by His blood—and He has made us to be a kingdom, priests to His God and Father—to Him be glory and the dominion forever and ever. Amen" (Revelation 1:5–6).

A LOOK BACK

The cosmic gamble failed. He who would not be God's willing servant is now God's unwilling prisoner. He who wished to strut about the world is now confined to the parameters of hell. He who wished to rule others now finds that he cannot rule himself.

The destruction of the Serpent in the lake of fire stands as a final witness to the fact that no creature who fights against the Creator will win. No will pitted against the will of God will ever find permanent fulfillment and freedom. God has proved that He alone rules, and beside Him there is no other.

The devil rules today, but only by divine decree. He tempts us, but only to the extent that God chooses to grant him his wish. He destroys, but only as God approves of such destruction. He stalks proudly about, but only as far as God will let him. He is unwilling to face the reality of his impending eternal humiliation and shame. He already knows what others might not: His present battles are but a charade on the cosmic stage. The outcome is certain and unavoidable.

Meanwhile, Satan exists as God's instrument of justice for the disobedient and God's means of purification for the obedient. Our war with him teaches us about the nature of sin, the holiness of God, and our own helplessness apart from Grace. Lucifer's fall gave our heavenly Father an opportunity to display limitless mercy toward us. He who rules all things by the counsel of His own will has triumphed, and we share His victory.

And you, my friend, can also share His victory if you transfer your trust to Christ, acknowledging your helplessness apart from

Him. Only personal faith in Christ can shield us from the wrath to come; only those who have faith in "the blood of the Lamb" can overcome the devil's fury. And overcome it, they will.

Oh, the depth of the riches both of the wisdom and the knowledge of God! How unsearchable are His judgments and unfathomable His ways! For who has known the mind of the Lord, or who became His counselor? Or who has first given to Him that it might be paid back to Him again? For from Him and through Him and to Him are all things. To Him be the glory forever. Amen. (Romans 11:33–36)

Soli Deo Gloria.

NOTES

Chapter 1

1. William Gurnall, *The Christian in Complete Armour: Daily Readings in Spiritual Warfare,* ed. James S. Bell (Chicago: Moody, 1995), reading for March 22.
2. Kenneth L. Woodward, "Do We Need Satan?" *Newsweek,* 13 November 1995, 64.
3. Ibid.
4. Ibid., 67.
5. Ibid., 64.
6. Gerald McGraw, "Is Your Devil Too Big?" *Alliance Life,* 27 February 1991, 9.

Chapter 3

1. Donald Grey Barnhouse, *The Invisible War* (Grand Rapids: Zondervan, 1965), 231–32.
2. Ibid.

Chapter 4

1. Marilyn Ferguson, *The Aquarian Conspiracy* (Los Angeles: Jeremy P. Tarcher, 1980), 23.
2. Annette Hollander, *How to Help Your Child Have a Spiritual Life* (New York: A&W, 1980), 31.
3. C. S. Lewis, *The Screwtape Letters* (New York: Macmillan, 1943), 39.
4. Nikos Kazantzakis, *The Last Temptation of Christ,* quoted in *AFA Journal,* July 1988, 22.
5. Allan Watts, *Beat Zen, Square Zen and Zen* (San Francisco: City Lights, 1959), 10.

Chapter 6

1. Frederick S. Leahy, *Satan Cast Out* (Carlisle, Pa.: Banner of Truth, 1975), 30.

Chapter 11

1. H. G. Wells, quoted by Constance Cumbey, *The Hidden Dangers of the Rainbow* (Lafayette, La.: Huntington House, 1983), 125.
2. Ibid.

Chapter 12

1. Jay Adams, *The Big Umbrella and Other Essays and Addresses* (Presb. & Reformed, 1973), 118.
2. J. Marcellus Kik, quoted in Frederick S. Leahy, *Satan Cast Out* (Carlisle, Pa.: Banner of Truth, 1975), 61.
3. Sir Francis Newport, *Knight's Master Book of New Illustrations* (Grand Rapids: Eerdmans, 1956), 159.